On the Wings of Isis:

Reclaiming the Sovereignty of Auset

a Girl God Anthology

Edited by Trista Hendren,
Susan Morgaine
and Pat Daly

Foreword by Jhenah Telyndru

Cover Art by Elisabeth Slettnes

ISBN: 978-82-93725-09-1

www.thegirlgod.com

Praise for On the Wings of Isis: Reclaiming the Sovereignty of Auset

"This is storytelling at its richest and most compelling. Collections like this one stand the test of time, persistently giving lie to pervasive anti-feminist mythologizing."
-Soraya Chemaly, Author of *Rage Becomes Her: The Power of Women's Anger*

"Inhale the mighty nectar of Isis in this empowering book, and utilize it to fuel your sovereign Queendom life and being!"
-SARK, Author/Artist of *Succulent Wild Woman*

Praise for Original Resistance: Reclaiming Lilith, Reclaiming Ourselves

"*Original Resistance* is an inspiring collection of essays, stories, and poems centered around Lilith, a timely symbol of women's resistance and self sovereignty. The diverse voices in this book create a powerful call to women to reclaim themselves and the spirit of Lilith, whose time has come."
-Sue Monk Kidd, Author of *The Invention of Wings*

"Everything my feminine soul has been thirsting for is contained in the brimming cup of this book. The Lilith archetype unleashes the wild heart, blows open the gates of the nondual mind, and blesses every cell of the holy, holy body. A fiery elixir of poetry and scholarship, myth and personal narrative, *Original Resistance* is a call to sacred action riding in on a wave of lovingkindness."
-Mirabai Starr, Author of *Wild Mercy*

"The original warrior goddess: Lilith. This anthology shows the re-awakening of the major female archetype of resistance movement against the roots of patriarchy. Through these diverse voices, listen to the murmur of a revolution that lives in the hearts of all women and is now bursting forth in a roar."
-HeatherAsh Amara, Author of *Warrior Goddess Training*

Girl God Books

Original Resistance: Reclaiming Lilith, Reclaiming Ourselves

There is, perhaps, no more powerful archetype of female resistance than Lilith. As women across the globe rise up against the patriarchy, Lilith stands beside them, misogyny's original challenger. This anthology—a chorus of voices hitting chords of defiance, liberation, anger and joy—reclaims the goodness of women bold enough to hold tight to their essence. Through poetry, prose, incantation, prayer and imagery, women from all walks of life invite you to join them in the revolutionary act of claiming their place—of reclaiming themselves.

Inanna's Ascent: Reclaiming Female Power

Inanna's Ascent examines how females can rise from the underworld and reclaim their power, sovereignly expressed through poetry, prose and visual art. All contributors are extraordinary women in their own right, who have been through some difficult life lessons—and are brave enough to share their stories.

Re-visioning Medusa: from Monster to Divine Wisdom

A remarkable collection of essays, poems, and art by scholars who have researched Her, artists who have envisioned Her, and women who have known Her in their personal story. All have spoken with Her and share something of their communion in this anthology.

New Love: a reprogramming toolbox for undoing the knots

A powerful combination of emotional/spiritual techniques, art and inspiring words for women who wish to move away from patriarchal thought. *New Love* includes a mixture of compelling thoughts and suggestions for each day, along with a "toolbox" to help you change the parts of your life you want to heal.

Jesus, Muhammad and the Goddess
More than 35 international contributors reflect on finding Goddess within (and without) Christianity and Islam.

Hearts Aren't Made of Glass
My Journey from Princess of Nothing to Goddess of My Own Damned Life—a memoir of sorts by Trista Hendren.

How to Live Well Despite Capitalist Patriarchy
A book challenging societal assumptions to help women become stronger and break free of their chains.

The Girl God
A book for children young and old, celebrating the Divine Female by Trista Hendren. Magically illustrated by Elisabeth Slettnes with quotes from various faith traditions and feminist thinkers.

Tell Me Why
A feminist twist of the creation story told with love from a mother to her son, in hopes of crafting a different world for them both. Written by Trista Hendren / Illustrated by Elisabeth Slettnes.

My Name is Medusa
The story of the greatly misunderstood Goddess, including why she likes snakes. *My Name is Medusa* explores the "scary" dark side, the potency of nature and the importance of dreams. Arna Baartz gorgeously illustrates this tale by Glenys Livingstone, teaching children (big and small) that our power often lies in what we have been taught to fear and revile.

My Name is Inanna
Tamara Albanna weaves the tale of Inanna's despair, strength and triumph—giving children of all ages hope that the dark times in life will pass. Arna Baartz illustrates this journey with gorgeous paintings of the owls, lions, stars, sun and moon that direct Her. *My Name is Inanna* is dedicated to Tamara's beloved homeland, Iraq—The Cradle of Civilization; the Land of the Goddess.

My Name is Lilith

Whether you are familiar with the legend of Lilith or hearing it for the first time, you will be carried away by this lavishly illustrated tale of the world's first woman. This creative retelling of Lilith's role in humanity's origins will empower girls and boys to seek relationships based on equality rather than hierarchy.

My Name is Isis

In this fresh look at the ancient Egyptian Goddess, Susan Morgaine reclaims Isis as The Great Mother Goddess and The Giver of Life, from whom all things come. Arna Baartz mystically illustrates Her as healer and protectress. *My Name is Isis* is a treasure box for children of all ages who want to draw close to this wise and nurturing Mother Goddess.

My Name is The Morrigan

The Morrigan remains one of the most misunderstood goddesses of the Celtic pantheon. Her mythology is a tangled web of various guises, deeds, and battles—and even her name is a bit of a mystery! Dive into the world of the Goddess of Death, and learn about what The Morrigan really has to teach us—and, maybe you'll find that She, and death, aren't so scary after all!

My Name is Goddess of Willendorf

Today more than ever, the image of the Goddess of Willendorf is a relevant one. Women and girls are bombarded with Photoshopped images of an "ideal" body shape that is quite literally unattainable. Remembering Willendorf's powerful story reminds us of the beautiful abundance of the female body, with all of her hills and valleys, lush softness, and fertility. You don't want to miss this body-positive celebration of the Great Mother Goddess!

Dedicated to the Memory of the Notorious, Sovereign Queen, Ruth Bader Ginsburg.

May her Memory be a Revolution.

Table of Contents

She of the Throne

Jhenah Telyndru

"Know that I am a mother and universal nature, mistress of all the elements, primordial principle of time, sovereign of all things spiritual, queen of the dead, oceans, and queen also of the immortals." –The Golden Ass, Lucius Apuleius

I was deeply honored when I was approached to write this foreword by Susan Morgaine – one of the editors of this anthology who is also a friend and Sister – but I was also unsure that I was the best person for this task. Celtic cultures have been the focus of my life's work and have informed my spiritual practice for over 30 years. Although I studied ancient Egypt while I was an archaeology student and have had several moving experiences with Isis in ritual contexts over the years, I do not have an active relationship with her as a divinity. Surely, I thought, it would make more sense for a devotee of Isis to write this foreword instead? However, when Susan Morgaine explained that this anthology was an exploration of Isis as a Goddess of Sovereignty, I could not help but say yes – and was quite excited to revisit her mythos from this perspective.

Sovereignty is a common folk motif found in the literary traditions of many Celtic lands – from the earliest Irish manuscripts, to later Welsh story cycles, and on into the Anglo-Norman development of Brythonic Arthurian legends. I have spent a lot of time researching the concept of Sovereignty, its socioreligious function, and the evolution of its meaning over time and across cultures. I have also worked to gain an understanding of how a relationship between women and Sovereignty can empower the practices of modern-day spiritual seekers and devotees of the Divine Feminine.

What I have learned from my years of engagement with Sovereignty from Celtic lore is that an excavation of the symbolic language embedded in the narratives of these tales reveals an alchemical formula which we can use to guide us through the profound psycho-spiritual transformations required to reclaim our personal Sovereignty. I define personal Sovereignty as "fully conscious self-determination." This is a state of being that requires an enormous degree of self-knowledge, particularly in regard to the recognition and acceptance of the parts of ourselves which are grounded in authenticity, as well as those which are mired in the illusions of Shadow. The seeking and reclamation of Sovereignty is a defining force in my work, and is a foundational tenet of the Avalonian Tradition as practiced by the Sisterhood of Avalon.

So what is Sovereignty?

In Celtic legend, the quest for Sovereignty is believed to have its origins in the pre-Christian past where a potential king would undertake a *hieros gamos*, or sacred marriage, with a representative of the land. Sometimes Sovereignty was a tutelary Goddess who appeared to the would-be-king in the form of a woman, while other traditions featured a totemic representation of Sovereignty as seen in the lore describing the ritual mating of Irish kings with a white mare, who was later sacrificed and eaten. The divinity of the Sovereignty figure is clearly acknowledged in early Irish myth; she often appears as a hideous hag who tests the worth of those who would be king. When she couples with the man she has found worthy – thereby granting him the right of rulership – she is transformed into a beautiful maiden; the land is likewise enlivened by the fertile energies arising from her union with the new king.

In Welsh tradition, the figure of Sovereignty shifts to become more subtextual; no longer overtly depicted as a Goddess as in

Ireland, Sovereignty is nonetheless embodied in the form of Otherworldly Queens and Fairy Brides. Early Arthurian legends see the regenerative powers of Sovereignty conferred through more symbolic means, as with Arthur's raid of the Otherworld to secure the cauldron of its chief, or the later hero's quests to find the Holy Grail in order to heal the wounded king and restore the Wasteland. In later Arthurian tales, the very concept of Sovereignty shifts in meaning; rather than functioning to grant a king rulership over the land, it represents the desire of women to obtain sovereignty over themselves.

The primary role of the Sovereignty Goddess is to protect and enliven her land. Often displaying a martial aspect, Sovereignty will incite warriors to battle in defense of her territory. She acts to ensure the fertility of the land by joining its fate with that of a worthy king or chieftain, so that the land will prosper as he prospers. The most prevalent type of Sovereignty figure in Celtic lore links a king's authority to the righteousness of his rule and the wholeness of his body. Because his fate is connected to that of his kingdom, a lawless king or one who is physically imperfect – either through illness or by way of a wound – creates an imbalanced relationship with the land that results in famine, disease, or war. When an imbalance is present, Sovereignty reverts to her hag form, and she seeks a new king to replace the old.

Another Sovereignty type sees the right to rule conferred upon a candidate who often proves his worth through a contest of arms, and upon whom rule is granted either seasonally or annually. This periodic or seasonal Sovereignty type is less common in Celtic traditions, but it is overwhelmingly the most prevalent Sovereignty motif found in the mythos of Ancient Near Eastern and Mediterranean cultures.

Kingly sacrifice and succession through combat are key themes in the seasonal Sovereignty motif, and is often compared with the

Roman legend of the *rex Nemorensis.* According to lore, the title of *rex Nemorensis* – the sacred king who served as priest of the Goddess Diana in her grove on the shores of Lake Nemi – was earned by the defeat and death of the previous priest. The challenger first earns the right to engage in this combat by obtaining a piece of the "golden bough" – perhaps a sprig of mistletoe growing on the trees in the sacred grove.

The tale of Diana's priesthood greatly influenced anthropologist James G. Frazer. In his seminal work, *The Golden Bough*, Frazer contends that the *rex Nemorensis* is an example of a widespread ancient practice of the annual sacrifice of a sacred king, who represents the archetype of the Dying God, a solar and agricultural divinity that dies every year and is reborn.

Although many of Frazer's theories are now outdated, he did recognize a pattern of ancient belief and historic folk practices that speak to the idea of the *eniautos daimon* – a spirit or character who embodies the annual cycles of nature and who often serves as a proxy sacrifice to ensure the balance of nature is maintained. Just as the *hieros gamos* connected the king to the land and ensured its fertility, so would the sacrifice of the year king ensure the bounty of the harvest. In both cases, it is the king's relationship with the Goddess of Sovereignty that is reflected in the turning of the seasons, while also ensuring the continued balance of the cyclic round.

With all of this as context, it was an immense joy to reread the myths of Isis with different eyes and an open heart. Although I recognize that there is so much more to be learned by a committed devotee with a well-established relationship with Isis, it was deeply satisfying to recognize the presence of the fundamental characteristics of the Sovereignty motif in her tales, and indeed, embodied by her very person. Even taken at the most rudimentary level, her very name – originally Auset, which means

"Throne" – suggests Isis' role as a Sovereignty Goddess. Indeed, the earliest images of Isis often depicted her crowned with the hieroglyph for throne as part of her headdress. However, rather than a direct embodiment of the land, Isis appears instead to be a divine personification of the throne – a quintessential manifestation of concept of Sovereignty itself.

Isis' role to preserve and maintain the divine royal lineage is a central theme in her mythos. Daughter of the Earth God, Geb and the Sky Goddess, Nut, Isis was married to her brother Osiris who ruled over Egypt as king. Gods marrying their siblings is not uncommon in mythologies around the world, as taboos against incest tended not to apply to divinities. However, following the example set by Isis and Osiris – from whom they claimed decent through Horus – Egyptian pharaohs married their sisters or other close female kin in order to preserve the purity of their divine bloodline. Just as the pharaoh is Horus in life and becomes Osiris in death, the queen was identified with Isis – the Wife, Mother, and Protector of the king.

Great of Magic, Isis was invoked as a fierce and loyal defender of the pharaoh; she enfolded him in her wings – protecting him as she did her husband Osiris, and held him her lap-throne – as when she suckled her son, Horus.

Isis and Osiris had two other siblings, Set and Nephthys, who were also husband and wife. Where Isis and Nephthys were often depicted working together harmoniously, Osiris and Set were constantly at odds with each other, such that Osiris came to represent ordered balance, while Set exemplified chaotic imbalance. Coveting his brother's throne, Set tricked Osiris into lying in a lead coffin, which Set then sealed and cast into the Nile, causing Osiris to drown. Although overcome with grief and shedding countless tears, Isis searched for her beloved until she found his body, which she must free from an enormous tree that has grown up around it. Before she was able to give Osiris a proper funeral, Set discovered where Isis had hidden the coffin among the reeds; in a fury, he tore his brother's body apart and scattered its pieces across the land. Resolute, Isis enlisted the aid of Nephthys, and together they painstakingly search for and gather together all of the pieces of his body, save one: Osiris' phallus, which had been eaten by a fish.

In order to make Osiris whole once more, Isis used her formidable magic to construct a new phallus for him. With everything now in place, the sisters bound the body back together in a process which can be seen as the mythic antecedent to mummification and Egyptian funerary practices. Empowered by her love and grief, the magic of Isis brings her husband back to life long enough to conceive a child by him. The spirit of Osiris then enters the Afterlife, where he becomes king. The son of Isis and Osiris is Horus, who is destined to fight and defeat his uncle in order to reclaim what is rightfully his. Through her actions, Isis preserves and protects the lineage of kings.

Like other Sovereignty Goddesses I have studied, Isis is a shape changer. She uses her magic to disguise herself as an old woman so she can be near Horus to help him in his battle with Set – how reminiscent of the hag in Celtic myth who tests the would-be king! Isis is also transformed by her grief, and along with Nephthys, the sisters are often depicted mourning over the body of Osiris in the form of kites – carrion-eating birds of prey whose cries sound like the wails of the bereaved. How like the association of crows and ravens with Celtic Sovereignty Goddesses such as the Morrigan, Badb, and Cathubodua!

Finally, there is a seasonal component present as well. The tears shed by Isis while mourning Osiris were so numerous, they caused waters of the Nile to rise and inundate the land. One of the central cosmological paradigms in Ancient Egyptian culture is the sense of order that arises from the annual flooding of the Nile. This overflow was both consistent and critical, for the rich soils it deposited when it overran its banks renewed the fertility of the land and insured the continued survival of the people of Egypt.

The death of Osiris resembles myths from other Ancient Near Eastern and Mediterranean cultures which feature an agricultural deity whose annual death ensures a bountiful harvest; along with this abundance, the God is said to rise again. In Egypt, however, Osiris does not return to life but rather takes his throne in the afterlife. As he does so, it is Isis' grief which causes the land's renewal. This is strongly reminiscent of the revitalization of the land that results from the sacred union of the king with the Goddess of Sovereignty in Celtic mythos.

This Dying God motif underscores many of the savior god cults originating in the Near East and the Mediterranean that enjoyed enormous popularity in the expanding Roman Empire, particularly in the 1st century CE. The Cults of Mithras, Dionysus, and the Eleusinian Mysteries of Demeter and Persephone offered initiatory experiences which promised renewal in the afterlife. It is around this time that the Cult of Isis, first popularized by the Greek-lineaged Ptolemaic dynasties in Egypt, began to spread throughout the Roman Empire, even into Roman Britain. Like the other popular cults with Mediterranean and Ancient Near Eastern origin, the veneration of Isis outside of Egypt was connected to her savior aspect – the promise of rebirth and eternal life in the otherworld.

As her worship spread, the domains over which Isis held power expanded as well. In addition to her roles in Egyptian religion, she became associated with the moon, the seasons of the year, the fertility of the Earth, and considered to be the force which controlled the patterns of the cosmos. A guardian of women in general, and mothers in particular, Isis was also invoked to protect ships and harbors, and to assist armies in their defense of their nations. She came to be known as Isis Myrionymos – She of Many Names.

I am fond of saying that myths endure because they have something to teach us. Becoming a Universal Goddess in ancient times, the continued popular and renewed devotion to Isis in the present day suggests that she has returned to our consciousness here and now because she holds necessary wisdoms. And just like the stories that have inspired me from Celtic traditions, I am moved by the way the tales of Isis provide us with a mythic map that can guide us in the direction of our own Sovereignty.

There are many ways to approach this Goddess and to engage with her stories; one such way is to look at her myths from a psycho-spiritual perspective. In her most ancient form as the embodiment of the throne of Egypt, Isis serves as the foundation upon which sovereignty is based. She supports and elevates the king, protects and nurtures his person, and ensures the righteous continuity of the royal lineage. She knows powerful magic, is a devoted partner and mother, and is capable of enduring love and unyielding grief.

Reflecting this dynamic within us, we can say that Isis represents the unconscious principle within our psyche, which is related to intuition, emotions, deep memory, and wisdom. Osiris therefore represents the conscious principle, related to the higher mind, cognition, and knowledge. Inseparable, even by death, the two of them create the sacred third: Horus, the crowned and conquering child, the unifying principle whose right eye is the sun and left eye is the moon. Set can be seen as representing the Shadow principle, lashing out from a place of pain and need, and whose bid to be in control results in the destruction and death of the creative principle.

When our conscious and unconscious selves are in balanced relationship with each other, we are able to act with sovereignty in the world, creating our reality in accordance with our will and as a reflection of our authentic selves. When outside forces and situations beyond our control shift us from our center, we experience imbalance. This imbalance can trigger our Shadow instincts – unconscious responses to challenges which are rooted in old wounds and unacknowledged shame – to rise up in reaction to these experiences. We become trapped in outmoded and destructive patterns, and thus imprisoned like Osiris in his coffin, we are deprived of the ability to respond with clarity or reason. We become lost in the watery realms of emotional attachment and unconscious reaction until we are overcome and shattered into pieces.

And yet, within us... arising from the depths of our grief, comes strength. An intuitive wisdom that both honors our pain and is able to harness its power to put ourselves back together again, piece by harrowing piece. This deep wisdom knows how to ask for help when needed, like Isis seeking the support of Nephthys, and is willing to embrace the Shadow in order to affect true and lasting healing. What results from this union is a new and precious source of light, a rekindling of the inner flame that allows us to see ourselves and the world with new eyes. Although we may yet mourn what has passed, when we enter into conscious partnership with our unconscious self the gifts that have been buried within us begin to rise to the surface. Thus acknowledged, these once-hidden gifts are carried forth by the waters of our intuitive selves. They spill over the earthen banks of our now-outgrown limitations and bring with them an abundance that reinvigorates our landscapes – both within us and around us.

Thus transformed, we experience a sense of greater wholeness as we enter into a balanced relationship with all aspects of our self once more. But we are not alone. Lovingly held in the lap of Isis Invicta – the Unconquered Isis – we are nurtured, strengthened and protected. Thus empowered, we are better able to stand against the challenges of Shadow when they again confront us, as inevitably as the flooding of the Nile and the turning of the seasons. Yet each time we move through this alchemical process – the *solve et coagula* of our spiritual rarefication and growth – we become more solidly anchored in our partnership with the Holy Throne that upholds us. And each time, we are more skillfully armed with the gifts we have found within us, allowing us to face our Shadow with ever-increasing consciousness in order to reclaim what is rightfully ours: the birthright of our Sacred Sovereignty.

Sovereign Unto Herself

Trista Hendren

> "Deep in the psyche even of great women, there has not been a female metaphor for greatness, for strength, for the wisdom which they themselves embodied. The female Deities had been so slandered, so stripped of essential integrity... this is not myopia. The millennia of patriarchal narrative has left our minds locked up, unable to grasp the Female Metaphor... that she may stand sovereign, not as greater than, but in and of herself: so that, when a woman or a man desires to express greatness, nobility, strength they are able to easily reach for a female image."
> -Glenys Livingstone, PhD[1]

Imagine for a moment a picture of your greatest hero. *Who is it?* Why is this person your hero? How does her life relate to yours? How have they influenced you?

Our heroes are important: They guide us to where we can go (if we dare) and save us from our own limiting beliefs about ourselves. *How do we guide our children to find role models who will empower them?*

Every woman I know who took Women's Studies in college talks about how their whole world sort of opened up with their first class. Why do we deprive our girls of this experience throughout most of their education? Is it possible more children would love going to school if it related back to them directly?

How can they have heroes that don't reflect who they are?

---

1 Livingstone, Glenys PhD. *PaGaian Cosmology: Re-inventing Earth-based Goddess Religion.* iUniverse, 2005.

The highlight of my son's second grade school year was a "Hero Speech." The kids researched various historical figures, picked the one that they identified with most strongly, continued to research that person more thoroughly, and finally wrote and presented a speech (in costume) to the entire second grade community, including parents and grandparents.

It was a wonderful project, and I was thrilled to see my son so engaged with his research on Benjamin Franklin. When he finally took the stage, he *was* Ben Franklin.

However, when I went into his classroom a few months before to celebrate his birthday, I was dismayed. I was only hearing about research on male heroes. The kids were allowed to ask anything of me about my son's very early years. The questions they came up with were both creative and fun to answer. I decided to ask a few questions of my own.

I asked if the kids could name some female heroes.

No one could name even one.

The teacher explained that they were somewhat limited because the project required that they research books dedicated to heroes at their appropriate reading level. Apparently there just were not enough books written for second graders about women in history.[2]

---

2 I tried to remedy this with my (younger) daughter by searching out our own books—which I read with her at home. *The Who Was/Is* Series was one of the best we found—and we read through all the books on Women. I wrote to the publisher to request that they publish an equal number of women but they never responded. Burleigh Muten's *Ten Thousand Names: Goddess Stories from Many Cultures* was the first Goddess book we found for children. Now that I have a younger niece and nephew, I can see there is greater selection of books for children about women, people of color and LGBQT people. Whether or not these books are read in schools remains a mystery to me.

The day of the speeches was a proud one. It was heartwarming to see all the kids dressed up in their costumes, filled with pride after months of mastering their presentations. As the children's speeches were delivered, I couldn't help notice the numbers of girls who were dressed as male heroes, giving brilliant speeches in men's words.

There was not a single boy, of course, who dressed as his female hero or spoke in her words. My heart ached for all the second grade girls. In fact, I felt very sad for every woman in that room.

I couldn't help but wonder why this is still happening.[3]

Fast-forward about a decade, and I don't see a lot of change. While we now live in 'progressive' Norway, to-date, my daughter has had one day (ONE DAY!) where they focused on women's history in school.

When she has brought up Goddesses in the schools of this secular country, she has been hushed. Even with a curriculum that teaches all the major world religions, Goddess is never mentioned.

Imagine a world where our daughters grew up knowing Her many names and rich history. Imagine a world where women did not spend their entire lives searching for their divinity.

As Simone de Beauvoir wrote 60 years ago, "Man enjoys the great advantage of having a god endorse the code he writes; and since man exercises a sovereign authority over women it is especially fortunate that this authority has been vested in him by the

---

For those of us who are grown, I highly recommend the work of anthology contributor Max Dashu, who has been restoring women's history for over 50 years through her Suppressed Histories Archives.

3 Adapted from an earlier essay published in *Elephant Journal* entitled "Women's Studies Must Start Earlier." June 15, 2012.

Supreme Being."[4] I believe the time of men's authority is over. He has colonized the female sex long enough. As Monica Sjöö and Barbara Mor wrote: "...the female sex has functioned as a colony of organized patriarchal power for several thousand years now. Our brains have been emptied out of all memory of our own cultural history, and the colonizing power systematically denies such a history ever existed. The colonizing power mocks our attempts to rediscover and celebrate our ancient matriarchies as realities. In the past, women have had to accept this enforced female amnesia as "normal"; and many contemporary women continue to believe the female sex has existed always... as an auxiliary to the male-dominated world order. But we continue to dig in the ruins, seeking the energy of memory; believing that the reconstruction of women's ancient history has a revolutionary potential equal to that of any political movement today."[5]

Mainstreaming women's ancient history is long-overdue. Gerda Lerner wrote, "Women's history is the primary tool for women's emancipation."[6] When women learn their rich HERstory, there is a significant shift that ripples through their entire way of be-ing.

This anthology is our attempt to bring back some of the ancient and suppressed wisdom—via the Goddess commonly known through much of the world as Isis.

Leslene della-Madre explained, "Philae in southern Egypt, home of the Temple of Isis, was, itself, a very popular pilgrimage site in the millennium preceding Jesus and continuing several centuries beyond his death. Isis was a female deity with origins in central Africa, or Nubia, and was known as a compassionate mother. In *dark mother,* Lucia [Chiavola Birnbaum, Ph.D.] cites the work of

---

4 de Beauvoir, Simone. *The Second Sex.* Vintage; First edition; 1960.

5 Sjöö, Monica and Mor, Barbara. *The Great Cosmic Mother: Rediscovering the Religion of the Earth.* HarperOne; 2nd edition; 1987.

6 Lerner, Gerda. *The Creation of Patriarchy.* Oxford University Press; Reprint edition, 1987.

leading nubiologist and archeologist, William Y. Adams, who considers Isis worship to be 'one of history's most important ideological transformations.' Adams further writes that Isis worship became 'the first truly international and supra-national religion' because pilgrims of all classes and nationalities, including Meriotes, Egyptians, Greeks, Romans, and desert nomads alike flocked to Her temple for healing and spiritual guidance. Isis veneration spread as far east as Afghanistan, to the Black Sea, as well as to what is now western Europe in Portugal and as far north as England. It is Her legacy that has been inherited by christianity as revealed in the icons of the Black Madonnas found all over Europe; Isis and Her son Horus suckling at Her breast are most likely the prototypes for Mary and Jesus."[7]

Restoring this much earlier deity to memory begins the restoration of everything that patriarchy attempted to destroy.

Marianna Delray wrote, "The decline in Isiac iconography can be explained by intolerance of pagan cults and their imagery by the early Christian doctrine. However, it is worth noting that during the early stages of Christianity, when the cult of Isis was still widespread, its practices were witnessed by the pilgrims such as Paul during his missionary journeys through the cities of the Empire. For this reason, it is compulsory that the concepts reminiscent of the Isiac worship such as salvation, suffering, purification and resurrection, were later identified in the New Testament. By the fourth century, Christianity was officially embraced by Rome and the worshippers of Isis and other pagan gods were kept from power, while the cohesion of the old religion rapidly disintegrated. In fifth century Alexandria, the public burning of the cult objects seized from the Isis sanctuary at Menouthis, marked the beginning of the process of collection and open destruction of all pagan images. Consequently, the temple of

---

7 della-Madre, Leslene. "The Luminous Dark Mother." *She Is Everywhere! Volume 3.* Edited by Mary Beth Moser and Mary Saracino. iUniverse, 2012.

Isis at Philae is often referred to as 'one of the last bastions of pagan worship in Egypt."[8]

Women have lost much of their divine heritage. It is important for each of us to see ourselves in the divine. We also must ensure that none of our sisters are left out in our individual attempts at empowerment. Patricia Monaghan explained, "There has never been only one religion of the goddess. Every continent, every culture, had its own vision of the way that divine feminine should be pictured. Each culture pictured her as one of their own. She was black in Africa, blonde in Scandinavia, round-faced in Japan, dark-eyed in India. For the goddess was the essence of woman's strength and beauty to each one of her daughters, so she had to look like them. When ancient women looked at their goddess, they saw themselves."[9]

One of my first introductions to the Divine Feminine was Patricia Lynn Reilly's book, *A God Who Looks Like Me*—and, it shook me to my core. I have come to realize over the years that we have a long way to go in the Goddess community in terms of representing all ages, sizes and colors of Divine Women. Representation is important—particularly when the Goddess being depicted is, in fact, Black.

bell hooks wrote, "Women need to know that they can reject the powerful's definition of their reality—that they can do so even if they are poor, exploited, or trapped in oppressive circumstances. They need to know that the exercise of this basic personal power is an act of resistance and strength. Many poor and exploited women, especially non-white women, would have been unable to develop positive self-concepts if they had not exercised their

---

8 Delray, Marianna. "Legacy of the Egyptian Goddess? A Retrospective Look at the Two Divine Mothers, Isis and Mary." Macquarie University; 2017.

9 Monaghan, Patricia. *The New Book of Goddesses & Heroines.* Llewellyn Publications; 3rd edition, 1997.

power to reject the powerful's definition of their reality."[10] And that is a *really* important thing to remember. Because, as Marion Woodman said, "When you're living your own reality, you become the sovereign of your own life."[11]

Given the fact that most of us are not taught anything other than white male history in school, it is important that we take up the task of educating ourselves. And each of us have considerable work to do. While I have been studying alternative narratives since college, I still have some major blind spots. Anthology contributor Tyreesha Garrett encouraged me to begin to dig deeper through the works of Anthony Browder. Recently Browder stated, "I know beyond a shadow of a doubt that when people of African ancestry are exposed to the truths that have been historically hidden away from us, it changes the way we see ourselves—it increases our level of respect for ourselves and those who look like us. It changes everything. And that is the reason why this information is still not being taught in schools to this very day."[12]

It is crucial to recognize that the Goddess many of us know as Isis is the ancient Nubian Goddess, Auset—who was later renamed by the Greeks. Contributor Olivia Church explains some of this process in her upcoming book: "From earth, sea, and sky, to life, death, and magic, Isis' powers became all encompassing. During the Graeco-Roman Period, starting in 332 BCE, Mediterranean culture flooded Egypt, bringing its Gods to Egypt and taking Egyptian Gods across the sea. The Greeks and Romans who travelled to Egypt interpreted Egyptian religion through their own eyes, thus merging and assimilating cultural ideas (Stadler, 2017). It is during this time that Isis underwent transformations which

---

10 hooks, bell. *Feminist Theory: From Margin to Center.* Routledge; 3 edition, 2014.

11 Woodman, Marion. Interview with Elizabeth Lesser. O, *The Oprah Magazine*, 2012.

12 Browder, Anthony T. "New Findings from Egypt & Sudan with Anthony T. Browder." *Rock Newman Show;* Sep 23, 2016.
See also: Mami Wata's *Africa's Ancient God/dess Unveiled Vol. I & II*

are recognisable to how we view her today (Bowden, 2010). The Greeks and Romans attributed new areas of influence and symbols to Isis, leading her to gain more and more epithets, until she was thus-named Isis myrionymos, or Isis of innumerable names (McCabe, 2007). At the height of this period there was little beyond her divine sphere of influence."[13]

Dr. Muata Abhaya Ashby has extensively explained how redressing misconceptions and errors around geography and traditions is necessary for world healing. "Ancient Egyptian culture and philosophy is crucial to the understanding of world history and spirituality. One of the misconceptions which is still promoted and prevalent in modern times is that Egypt is not a part of, or located on, the continent of Africa. Rather, it is espoused that Egypt is in the Middle East. This information is incorrect, as Egypt is where it has always been located, though in history it extended beyond its current margins, in the northeast corner of the African Continent. Further, it is widely believed by others that even though Egypt may be in Africa, that it was not an African country, and still others may agree that it was an African country, but not originally founded and populated by "black" African people... These errors must be redressed in order for humanity to move forward... Africa provides a common ground, literally and figuratively, for humanity to come together as... the spiritual roots of all religions and spiritual traditions can be traced there as well... The world community needs to have the knowledge of its African human and spiritual origins so that Africa can take its rightful place as the 'parent' of all humanity. It is important to understand that the names of the Ancient Egyptian divinities which have been used widely in Western literature and by Western scholars are actually Greek interpretations of the Kamitan (Ancient Egyptian) names."[14]

---

13 Church, Olivia. *Isis: Great of Magic, She of 10,000 Names*. Pagan Portals series, Winchester, Moon Books; 2021 (p. 42).

14 Ashby, Dr. Muata Abhaya. *The African Origins of African Civilization, Religion, Yoga Mysticism Ethics Philosophy and a History of Egyptian Yoga (Book 1 - Part 1)*. Sema Institute, 2011.

Acknowledging and revering our ancient Mother Auset is an important step toward reconciliation.

Lucia Chiavola Birnbaum Ph.D. wrote, "Slave traders, slaveholders, and imperialists (european, arab, and north american) enslaved Africa's peoples. African resources were stolen, african treasures sacked, icons and other art objects were looted and taken away. African traditions were appropriated, destroyed, distorted, or suppressed. What remains in Africa today is what could not be stolen: the memory of the dark mother in rock engravings, cave paintings, other art, and rituals."[15]

It is time to bring these images and rituals back in the public eye.[16] Art and rituals are perhaps even more important than the written word. There is no denying the pull of ancient symbols on our psyches. They go beyond 'logic' into the deep recesses of the heart. When we take this a step further and incorporate rituals honoring the Divine Female, we begin to heal ourselves.

Isis remains a powerful archetype for many women throughout the world. Understanding where She originated from is critically important. Elinor W. Gadon wrote, "While the Goddess indeed had many names, many manifestations throughout human history, she is ultimately one supreme reality. Only after the patriarchal Indo-Europeans overthrew the cultures where the Goddess had flourished from earliest times and imposed the worship of their sky gods was her identity fractured into myriad goddesses, each with an all-too-human personality. We know these goddesses best from Greek and Roman mythology."[17] We also know that these myths are usually distorted by patriarchal thought.

---

15 Birnbaum, Lucia Chiavola Ph.D. "African Dark Mother - Oldest Divinity We Know." Authors Choice Press, 2001.

16 See *The Sacred Magic of Ancient Egypt: The Spiritual Practice Restored* (2002) and by Rosemary Clark (Llewellyn Publications).

17 Gadon, Elinor W. *The Once and Future Goddess: A Sweeping Visual Chronicle of the Sacred Female and Her Reemergence in the Cult.* HarperOne; 1989.

Goddesses have been defragramented and disempowered throughout modern history. I have come to realize during the course of putting this anthology together that we still have quite a lot of digging to do. My hunch is that we are missing out on the full divinity of Auset when we only focus on what we have learned about Isis. There is likely a richer, untainted HERstory still hidden which must be brought to the forefront.

That said, I want to acknowledge the complexity of this. How do you even begin to reconfigure a Goddess that most of the western world knows by a different name?

I was oblivious to the name change when we began this book. We amended the name of the anthology to include both names—and extended the timeline for publication so that I could re-write this introduction. At times, this book felt messy and tedious. I was mad at myself and at my ignorance—and even at the entire educational system. My sisters walked me through it with great insight and compassion. Although I have acknowledged them at the end of the book, I would like to give special thanks to contributors Tyreesha Garrett, Olivia Church, Sharon Smith and Arlene Bailey for helping me sort this out. And of course to my mother, Pat Daly who edited my drafts tirelessly.

I put out these anthologies, not because I have all the answers, but because I am searching for answers myself. I want to unlock all that has been buried in our world regarding the divine feminine. I am so grateful for each of the sisters who brought this anthology to life. I learned and healed so much from each unique share.

May the words and art within this anthology uncover what patriarchy has tried to bury—and may every woman become sovereign unto herself through the wisdom of The Goddess of Ten Thousand Names.

A Note About Styles, Preferences—and Names

Trista Hendren

On the Wings of Isis contains a variety of writing styles from women around the world. Various forms of English are included in this anthology and we chose to keep spellings of the writers' place of origin to honor/honour each woman's unique voice.

It was the expressed intent of the editors to not police standards of citation, transliteration and formatting. Contributors have determined which citation style, italicization policy and transliteration system to adopt in their pieces. The resulting diversity is a reflection of the diversity of academic fields, genres and personal expressions represented by the authors.[18]

Mary Daly wrote long ago that, "Women have had the power of naming stolen from us."[19] The quest for our own naming, and our own language, is never-ending, and each of us attempts it differently.

Lucia Chiavola Birnbaum, Ph.D. noted: "In previous books, I adopted the convention of european feminists and other democratic groups who remove capitals as a nonviolent way of toppling hierarchy, or the power over expressed in sexism, racism, homophobia, imperialism, and other expressions of destructive arrogance and ignorance that are often a cover for fear... Consistency is not a characteristic of times of rapid transition. I may want to depose all capitals but my publishers capitalized and uncapitalized as they saw fit... I cannot, retrospectively, change

18 This paragraph is borrowed and adapted with love from *A Jihad for Justice: Honoring the Work and Life of Amina Wadud*. Edited by Kecia Ali, Juliane Hammer and Laury Silvers.

19 Daly, Mary. *Gyn/Ecology: The Metaethics of Radical Feminism*. Beacon Press, 1990.

titles, nor tamper with what other people say, nor change their capitalization or punctuation to mine.[20] We have left works sited in this anthology as they were originally published.

Personally, I tend to only uncapitalize male names, such as god, while capitalizing female names, such as Goddess. It is inconsistent, as I am well aware, but that is what feels intuitively *right* to me, in terms of toppling the male preference I grew up with. As Normandi Ellis wrote, "We have to steal back the words of power of Isis in order to summon up the guts to declare out loud who we are, why we are here and what it is we want."[21]

The editors wish to note that the Goddess we know more familiarly as the Egyptian Goddess Isis stems back to the Nubian Goddess Auset, also often spelled Aset or Ast. Contributors to the anthology have referred to Her by both names and various spellings of Ast/Aset/Auset.

If you find that a particular writing doesn't sit well with you, please feel free to use the Al-Anon suggestion: "Take what you like, leave the rest!" That said, if there aren't at least several pieces that challenge you, we have not done our job here.

Mohja Kahf wrote:

> "All women speak two languages: the language of men and the language of silent suffering.
> Some women speak a third, the language of queens."[22]

May we all learn to speak the language of Queens.

---

20 Birnbaum, Lucia Chiavola Ph.D. *The Future Has an Ancient Heart: Legacy of Caring, Sharing, Healing, and Vision from the Primordial African Mediterranean to Occupy Everywhere*. iUniverse, 2012.

21 Ellis, Normandi. *Dreams of Isis: A Woman's Spiritual Sojourn*. Quest Books; 1995.

22 Kahf, Mohja. *E-mails from Scheherazad.* University Press of Florida; 1st edition, 2003.

Auset / High Priestess Arcana II

Max Dashu

Isis of 10,000 names the Nubian great goddess: Mother of the Gods, Giver of Life, Maker of the Sunrise, in this her name Weret hekau, the Great Enchantress, She Who Is Strong of Tongue, knowing many words of power.

As the star Sirius, her rising with the sun signals a new year and the fertilizing floodtide of the Nile. So Auset was also praised as Opener of the Year, Creatrix of the Nile Inundation, Lady of Abundance, Lady of Green Crops and of Bread.

Auset holds the Ankh, symbol of life, and the sistrum of Kemetic temple dancers.

She wears the horned solar disc of Het-Heru (Hathor) and the vulture crown of Mut (the Mother).

Auset is clothed in the night sky, her hips encircled by the red belt of the Mother's womb, enclosed by the Knot of Isis.

Excerpted from: *Deasophy: Coloring Book of Goddesses .:. Spirits .:. Ancestors* - Icons from the Suppressed Histories Archives, with drawings and commentary by Max Dashu

Hear Our Cries: An Invocation

Arlene Bailey

Oh Great Mother
Blessed Isis
You who found the lost
pieces of your beloved,
You who made whole again
that which you adored,
hear the cries of your
descendants, your
daughters and sons.

Hear the cries of our
waters and lands,
flowers and trees
and the animals.
We have become
dismembered parts,
Death wraiths walking.

Blessed Isis
Powerful Ancestral Creatrix
We call you to work your
magic upon us, reconnecting
that which is precious,
that which is beautiful,
that which is essential,
that which is dying.

We implore you to protect
the very existence of
All that exists in this time,
for Set walks among us still
dismembering
all that is Good,
all that is Sacred,
piece by piece by piece

Oh Great Mother
Blessed Isis
Queen of the All
Queen of Magic
Work this mystery upon us now,
gather the pieces of what's left,
there's not much and soon
there will be nothing.

Great Mother
Blessed Isis
Queen of the All
We are dead and dying
as we call out your name
imploring you to find us,
collecting our disparate parts.

Oh Great Mother
Protectress of the Dead and Dying
Death Crone
Breathe life back into us
before it's too late.

Great and Powerful Isis
We are your beloved Osiris
and our time is running out.
Set grows stronger as families
are torn apart, children starving
and dying, raped and sold, while
fires rage and destroy the land,
contaminating the waters, stopping
their flow as billions of animals die
and others go extinct.

Set is chopping it... us...
into pieces and your beloveds,
especially your daughters –
for Set's minions target them
and the land the most –
are raped, tortured and murdered
and will be no more.

Great Cosmic Mother
You who carry the power of alchemy
breathe life back into all that is dying.
You who create life from death and
wear the ankh – symbol of immortal life –
teacher of women and women's ways –
You who are the sun and moon, earth and stars
shelter us in your great wings as you
reweave a new world, a new way of being.

I call You forth by your names!

Auset Isis!

Great Mother!

Sovereign Queen!

Witch of the Night!

Keeper of Magic!

Goddess and Crone of the
Mysteries of Life and Death!

Alchemist!

Thou Who is All that has been,
Is and Shall be!

Thou most Holy!

Powerful Auset Isis
I call you forth as *Reckoner*
to hold accountable those
responsible for the desecration
of all that is sacred and holy,
beautiful and life-giving.

Oh Great Queen
I call you forth to restore
the Sovereignty of your
daughters, your sons, the
Sovereignty of the Land.

Powerful and Most Holy Isis
We are your beloved Osiris

and our time is running out.
Hear My...
Our...
Prayers.

Before it's too late.

Duwa Auset, Duwa[23]

Hear Our Cries: An Invocation by Arlene Bailey, ©2020

---

23 *Duwa Auset, Duwa –Thou are Goddess the most High (Khemetic)*

Queen of Herself

Arlene Bailey

Alkimia

Arlene Bailey

I am an alchemist
travelling between the
worlds of dark and light –
a phoenix born of fire.
Curious, creative, passionate,
wild and free,
I am a sovereign being
walking this earth as
Woman,
Queen,
Magick Maker,
Goddess of the Dark Mysteries,
Great Mother of All.
Some call me Auset.
Some Isis.
I am the genesis of life itself
and the passage to the afterworld.
I Have Been.
I Am.
I Will Always Be.

Goddess Isis Archetypes and Attributes[24]

Syma Kharal

Origin: Egyptian

Also Called: Auset, Aset, Ast, Est, Iset

Name Meanings: Throne, Queen, Mother of all Gods and Goddesses, One and All Goddess, Goddess of Ten Thousand Names, Great Goddess

Attributes:

1. Goddess of all
2. Magic
3. Alchemy
4. Healing
5. Manifesting
6. Love
7. Royalty
8. Mourning
9. Queen of heaven
10. Queen of the underworld

---

24 This chapter is from Syma Kharal's book, *Goddess Reclaimed: 13 Initiations to Unleash Your Sacred Feminine Power,* which thoroughly discusses 13 Goddesses and culminates with an extensive chapter on Isis. To compliment the flow of this anthology, we chose to break the chapter up into 4 parts.

11. Resurrection
12. Renewal
13. Afterlife
14. Ritual
15. All elements and cosmos
16. Creation
17. Transformation
18. Initiation
19. Civilization
20. Law and justice
21. Commerce
22. Success
23. Language
24. Protection
25. Sacred mysteries
26. Dreams and goals
27. Prophesy
28. High Priestess
29. Sacred chants
30. Perseverance
31. Courage
32. Sacred sexuality
33. Karmic/past-life healing

34. Miracles
35. Marriage
36. Motherhood
37. Leadership
38. Fertility
39. Abundance
40. Spring
41. Beauty
42. Feminine empowerment
43. Women's wisdom
44. Changing fate/fortune
45. Ascension
46. Higher/spiritual perception

Self-actualization

1. Throne
2. Crown (sun disk in the center of cow horns)
3. Wings
4. Long sheath dress
5. Breastfeeding mother
6. Milk
7. Blood
8. *Ankh* (cross with loop/oval head)

9. *Tyet* (sacred knot symbol/amulet)
10. *Menat* necklace
11. *Sistrum* (rattle)
12. Sirius (Sopdet)
13. Lotus flower
14. Sycamore tree
15. Papyrus
16. Sun and moon
17. The Nile
18. Hieroglyphics
19. Perfume bottles
20. Altar
21. Kite or swallow
22. Vulture
23. Scorpion
24. Cow

Chakras: All seven (root, sacral, solar plexus, heart, throat, third eye, and crown)

Elements: All (water, air, earth, fire, and ether)

Essential Oils:

1. Frankincense
2. Sandalwood

3. Lotus
4. Jasmine
5. Cedarwood
6. Rose
7. Patchouli
8. Cinnamon
9. Eucalyptus
10. Lavender
11. Fennel
12. Geranium
13. Vetiver
14. Myrrh
15. Fig

Colors:

- Gold
- Silver
- Blue
- Red

Crystals:

- Lapis lazuli
- Red jasper
- Clear quartz

- Carnelian
- Moonstone
- Apache tear
- Obsidian

Archetype in Balance:

1. Empowered
2. Whole
3. Practices self-love and acceptance
4. Is always willing to grow
5. Takes responsibility for one's healing
6. Dedicated to serving others
7. Allows one to be supported
8. Loyal
9. Decisive
10. Benevolent
11. Generous
12. Charismatic
13. Fair/just
14. Dedicated to one's purpose
15. Hones and expresses one's talents
16. Shares one's gifts with confidence
17. Has a deep and rich spiritual life

18. Is the authority in one's life
19. Leads and inspires others with grace
20. Protects what one values and cherishes
21. Embraces change and transformation
22. Values spiritual and earthly life equally
23. Treats oneself with care and respect
24. Is compassionate with oneself and others
25. Gets help when one needs it
26. Harnesses one's spiritual gifts
27. Co-creates the life one desires and deserves with inspired action
28. Lives a healthy lifestyle
29. Is resourceful and self-sufficient
30. Embraces and honors all of oneself
31. Has a supportive tribe
32. Seeks and intends everyone's highest good
33. Loves being a woman
34. Appreciates one's feminine gifts
35. Is the Queen of one's life

Archetype out of Balance:

- Has difficulty receiving intuitive guidance
- Doesn't trust and follow inner guidance

- Stagnant
- Uninspired
- Gives power away
- Insecure
- Confused
- Lacks focus
- Aggressive
- Martyr
- Victim
- Tries to rescue others
- Has spiritual ego
- Ungrounded
- Can isolate self
- Projects on others
- Doesn't take responsibility for personal wounds
- Lacks self-awareness
- Resists pain and growth
- Hides spiritual side out of fear of judgment or condemnation
- Can have social anxiety
- Can misuse spiritual power
- Manipulative

- Cunning
- Stubborn
- Power-hungry

Creating Balance:

- Maintain your own identity in relationships.
- Empower rather than enable others.
- Trust that everyone is capable of learning their own lessons.
- Respect each person's unique spiritual journey and life path.
- Cultivate your power from within, from your Sovereign nature.
- Use your power consciously and wisely.
- Trust and follow your intuition.
- Prioritize sacred self-care.
- Ask for your needs to be met.
- Assert your boundaries with graceful firmness.
- Get further training to awaken your spiritual gifts.
- Value your time and talents; charge a fair fee for sharing your gifts (or require an energy exchange).
- Consider other's advice, but make your own decisions in the end.
- Look for the lesson in life challenges.

- Create and tend to an altar for your spiritual practices.
- Allow yourself to shine like the star Sirius in the midnight sky.
- Explore past life work to heal karmic patterns and awaken your ancient knowledge and gifts.
- Command rather than demand respect.
- Respect yourself and others.
- Stay true to your purpose and dreams.
- Celebrate your good with others.
- Celebrate others' success.
- Collaborate with others.
- Practice self-love and compassion.
- Invest in the best quality products you can afford.
- Treat yourself to luxurious experiences within your means.
- Make the mundane sacred through ritual and ceremony.
- Use mantras and sacred words, prayers, chants, affirmations, and spells for healing and manifesting.
- Tend to what you love and value.
- Forgive and move forward.
- Hold space for yourself and others.
- Create sacred sisterhood by connecting with and supporting like-minded women and allow yourself to be supported in turn.

- Attend or host spiritual gatherings, especially women's circles.
- Know that you lead and serve best by being your fullest, truest self.
- Manifest your dreams with spiritual tools (visualization, meditation, prayer, mantras, crystals) and inspired strategic action.
- Embrace challenges as initiations into a higher level of ascension into your power, wisdom, and sovereignty.

Associated Goddesses: All Goddesses, but most specifically:

- Hathor (Egyptian)
- Maat (Egyptian)
- Sekhmet (Egyptian)
- Ishtar (Mesopotamian)
- Aphrodite (Greek)
- Athena (Greek)
- Hecate (Greek)
- Demeter (Greek)
- Hera (Greek)
- Hestia (Greek)
- Artemis (Greek)
- Devi (the Indian/Hindu All-Goddess)
- Astarte (Middle Eastern)

- Mother Mary (Christian)
- Mary Magdalene (Christian)
- Brigid (Celtic)
- Sophia (Gnostic)
- Kuan Yin (Chinese)
- Tara (Tibetan)
- Yemanya (Yoruba)
- Oshun (Yoruba)
- Eagle Woman (Aztec)
- Inanna and Ereshkigal (Sumerian)

Goddess of 10,000 Names

Arna Baartz

Illustration from *My Name is Isis* by Susan Morgaine.

Agency in the Face of Adversity

Olivia Church

Aset is a Goddess (a *Netjeret* in ancient Egyptian) with an extraordinary history, reaching back to at least the 5th Dynasty of Egypt's Old Kingdom over 4400 years ago, so far as written words can tell.[25] Aset wove her magic through ancient Egyptian culture for millennia, before the Greeks and Romans came to adopt her into their own religious systems, naming her "Isis". The image we have of her today is highly influenced by this Graeco-Roman form, which is in part because this period of time (332 BCE – 395 CE) was when her cults were at their most widespread both within and beyond Egypt. On the other hand, however, such reinterpretations have perpetuated a Mediterranean portrait of Aset, following the antiquarian trend of claiming Egyptian heritage for Eurocentric narratives of history. It is therefore essential that we collectively reclaim Aset's North African Egyptian origins in order to restore both her sovereignty as a Goddess and the sovereignty of North African cultural heritage. For this reason, I will refer to her as Aset for the remainder of this article, rather than Isis.

Aset is a Goddess who has endured through literally thousands of years' worth of cultural exchanges. She has survived beyond the closure of her ancient temples and proves to be one of the most beloved Goddesses revived from the ancient world today. Aset's popularity stems not only from her magical allure, exotic beauty, or shining regalia. She remains popular today due to her ability to empathise with the human condition, as well as her indominable sense of autonomy and personal agency. According to her ancient mythology, Aset was not a Goddess who surrendered to the great woes thrown her way: To modern readers at least, it is clear that

25 Tower Hollis, S. (2009) Hathor and Isis in Byblos in the Second and First Millennia BCE. *Journal of Ancient Egyptian Interconnections.* 1 (2), 1-8 (p.1).

Aset takes control of her situation and demonstrates how to handle challenges like a queen!

It is often said that knowledge is power, and this is certainly true according to ancient Egyptian religion and mythology. Aset was destined to become the divine queen of Egypt through her marriage to the God Wesir (known to the Greeks as Osiris), which conferred upon her significant authority and power;[26] however, though a modern feminist reading one could suggest that Aset was not content to possess power which was reliant upon her marriage to a king. Instead she sought sovereignty in her own right by becoming skilled in magic and rich in wisdom. As a result, according to the *Coffin Texts*, Aset became renowned as a Goddess who knew everything "in the sky and on the earth."[27] The one thing that she did not know, however, was the true name of the Creator God Ra, a fact of which she was considerably aware.

The myth of Ra's Secret Name describes how the God kept his true name hidden from all other creations in existence, to prevent any from causing him harm.[28] The Egyptians believed that written and spoken words held great power and could be used to manipulate things in real life; this extended to someone's name, their *ren,* which was considered a living part of them, as much as their physical or spiritual bodies.[29] This meant that the possessor of Ra's true name would have the power to manipulate the Creator God himself, for good or for ill. Without possession of his true name, no creature could harm him, except from himself. Aset's intentions were not to cause the Creator harm, but to acquire his name, and the power it provided. A spell recorded in the *Turin Magical*

26 Wilkinson, R. (2003) *The Complete Gods and Goddesses of Ancient Egypt.* London, Thames & Hudson (p.146).

27 *Coffin Texts* 411; translation from, Faulkner, R. (2007) *The Ancient Egyptian Coffin Texts.* Oxford, Aris et Phillips.

28 Ritner, R. (2008) *The Mechanics of Ancient Egyptian Magical Practice.* Chicago, The Oriental Institute of the University of Chicago (p.22).

29 Ikram, S. (2003) *Death and Burial in Ancient Egypt.* London, Pearson Education (pp.24-26).

Papyrus tells us how Aset, intent on obtaining this secret name, concocted a plan to trick Ra into revealing it willingly to her.[30] Her plan was thus: To covertly collect some of Ra's spittle as he slept and magically form a serpent with it. The serpent would then bite Ra necessitating that Aset come to his aid offering to heal him. In turn, she would cry out, if only she knew the name of the being which had harmed him! Inevitably Aset's plan succeeded. Ra screamed in agonising pain following the serpent's bite, whereupon the Goddess ran to his side offering to help him. Ra provided numerous alternative epithets to no avail. It became clear to him that he had no other option but to concede to Aset's request.[31] The tale ends with Aset learning his secret name, obtaining its power, and restoring Ra to health. Hereafter, she is known by the title, *'weret hekau'* or 'Great of Magic'.[32]

This myth demonstrates how, from the very beginning, Aset sought power for herself through the pursuit of knowledge. She fixed her attention upon her goal and set to achieve it by any means necessary. Her prioritisation of knowledge, above other forms of power, would prove to be invaluable to her throughout the rest of her mythology. She chose to empower herself, not only by her regal title, but in her embodied choices.

The story of Aset and Wesir is a famous one, which cannot be explored in full detail here; however, a summary of key moments serve to provide a portrait of Aset's sense of agency. The first section of stories belonging to this mythic cycle survive through the combination of the Egyptian *Stela of Amenmose* and the retellings of the Greek authors, Plutarch and Diodorus Siculus.[33]

30 Pinch, G. (2006) *Magic in Ancient Egypt.* London, British Museum Press (pp.29-30).

31 Pinch (2006), pp.70-71.

32 *Papyrus Ebers* 2; translation from, Lesko, B. (1999) *The Great Goddesses of Egypt.* Norman, University of Oklahoma Press (p.170).

33 *Stela of Amenmose;* Assmann, J. (2005). *Death and salvation in ancient Egypt* (trans. D. Lorton). Ithaca, Cornell University Press; McCabe, E. (2008) *An examination of the Isis Cult with Preliminary Exploration into New*

The myth unfolds with Aset and Wesir ruling as successful divine monarchs over Egypt. Their brother Sutekh (Greek Seth), God of the desert and thunderstorms,[34] was jealous of Wesir's good fortune, and from the Middle Kingdom onwards, Egyptian sources assert that Sutekh was responsible for the death of Wesir.[35] The most common method recorded is that Sutekh tricked Wesir into entering a coffin whereupon he sealed the lid and cast him into the Nile to drown.[36] Aset was stricken with grief. She had just lost her beloved in a devastating act of violence at the hands of her own family. The story goes on to describe how Aset fled in search for Wesir's body and "did not rest until she found him..."[37] Even as a mourning widow Aset did not succumb to her grief, determined to recover Wesir's coffin. She trusted in her own magic to help him somehow and could not allow Sutekh to get away with his terrible crime.

Plutarch elaborates, explaining how Aset recovered the coffin containing Wesir's body in the ancient city of Byblos, in modern day Lebanon.[38] Aset brought his body back home to Egypt, but was unsuccessful in hiding it from the knowledge of Sutekh. Furious with Aset's audacity to retrieve the body, Sutekh proceeded to viciously tear it into thirteen pieces and scatter them across Egypt.[39] Although a devastating blow, Aset still refused to give in. Accepting that she needed help, she called upon her twin sister Nebet-hut (Greek Nephthys) to retrieve each part and perform a funerary rite which would restore Wesir back to life, long enough to conceive an heir. This is beautifully

---

Testament Studies. Maryland, University Press of America (pp.5, 13).

34 Pinch, G. (2002) *Egyptian Mythology. A guide to the Gods, Goddesses and Traditions of Ancient Egypt.* Oxford, Oxford University Press (p.192).

35 Hart, G. (2005) *The Routledge dictionary of Egyptian gods and goddesses* (second edition), London, Routledge (p.117).

36 McCabe (2008), p.6.

37 *Stela of Amenmose;* translation from, Assmann (2005), p.24.

38 Plutarch, *Isis and Osiris,* 14-17; Plutarch, *Moralia, Vol. 5, 'Isis and Osiris'.* trans. F. C. Babbitt (1936). London, Harvard University Press.

39 Lesko (1999), p.162.

illustrated on numerous reliefs, with Aset in kite form hovering above Wesir's body as Nebet-hut weeps.[40] Though it may appear that Aset is the epitome of resourcefulness and strength, she is not devoid of feeling. The tears shed by her during this time were enough to cause the Nile to flood its banks:

> *"...I desire to see thee!*
> *I am thy sister Aset, the desire of thine heart,*
> *(Yearning) after thy love whilst thou are far away;*
> *I flood this land (with tears) to-day..."*[41]

The cries of grief expressed by Aset and Nebet-hut as they searched for Wesir were akin to the screeching of kites seeking carrion.[42] Wesir's funerary rites were likewise desperately sad:

> *"and our eyes are weeping for thee,*
> *the tears burn.*
> *Woe (is us) since our Lord was parted from us!"*[43]

The events described above serve to demonstrate three key things: First, Aset recognises that sometimes even powerful individuals, such as herself, need help from others; she is not too proud to ask for this and trusts her sister (who is also her enemy's wife) to support her.[44] Second, once again, Aset refuses to give up when something traumatic happens to her and despite the turmoil, she is able to think rationally about how to handle her

---

40 Wilkinson (2003), p.147.

41 *Bremner-Rhind Papyrus* 3:13-16; translation from, Faulkner, R. (1936) The Bremner-Rhind Papyrus: I. A. The Songs of Isis and Nephthys. *The Journal of Egyptian Archaeology.* 22 (2), pp.121-140. Please note that I have replaced the quote's original "Isis" with "Aset" for consistency.

42 Bailleul-LeSuer, R. (2012) Birds in Creation Myths. In: Bailleul-LeSuer, R. (eds.) *Between Heaven and Earth. Birds in Ancient Egypt.* Chicago, Oriental Institute Museum Publications, pp.131-134 (p.134).

43 *Bremner-Rhind Papyrus*, 3:17-19; Faulkner (1936), pp.121-140.

44 Pinch (2002), p.171.

situation. Refusing to allow Sutekh to get away with his actions, Aset knew that in order to regain her sovereignty she would need to produce an heir who would challenge Sutekh's claim to the throne. Third, in addition to displaying an iron-will to carry on, to fight against her aggressor, and to regain her authority, this queen remains in touch with her emotions. She cries literal floods of tears, she screams in rage, and is comforted by her sister. This shows how being in touch with one's emotions does not compromise one's strength in the face of adversity.

The subsequent events of Aset's mythology detail the birth of her son Heru (Greek Horus) and his subsequent confrontation with Sutekh. As a mother, Aset expresses her fear over her infant's survival, a concern which she would have shared with Egyptian mothers in antiquity, as well as many around the world today. Her vulnerability is described in the *Metternich Stela*, where Aset desperately seeks a cure for Heru, who has been bitten by a venomous creature.[45] With the assistance of Djehuty (Greek Thoth), God of wisdom,[46] Aset heals her son of his wound, powerfully declaring "every reptile with stings listens to me... Aset, great of magic..."[47] Aset is thus able to claim her power and authority, earnt through her seeking knowledge and help from allies.

Though the stories relating to the *Contendings of Heru and Sutekh* concern the activities of their titular Gods, Aset exerts her will throughout. This narrative explores Egyptian questions regarding royal inheritance, asking who is more entitled, the experienced twin brother of the deceased king, or the king's young son? To readers, the answer to this is clear from the start, with Aset's name translating to "throne" and written with the throne

45 Pinch (2006), p.144.

46 Pinch (2002), p.202.

47 Scott, N. (1951) The Metternich Stela. *The Metropolitan Museum of Art Bulletin*. 9 (8), pp.201-217 (pp.210-211). Again I have replaced the quote's original "Isis" with "Aset".

hieroglyph itself.[48] Heru is the one who, having sat upon the lap of Aset as an infant, has the direct right to sit upon the throne of Egypt as its king; however, though this right may seem obvious, according to the *Papyrus Chester* Beatty, the matter was not so straightforward.

It was decreed by the Divine Court of Gods, that Heru and Sutekh would have to fight for their claim to the throne through a series of contests. This announcement greatly angered Aset, who openly expressed her rage at the injustice. Attempting to silence her, Sutekh banished Aset from the island where the Gods were convening, instructing the God Nemty to deny her passage. It would not be true to Aset's character if she had allowed herself to back down and be silenced; therefore, making use of her cunning, Aset disguised herself as an old woman to trick Nemty into allowing her passage.[49] Upon her return she worked tirelessly to support Heru in his trials against Sutekh. Heru may appear to be the hero of the ancient narrative, but he could not have succeeded against his uncle without the aid of his mother's magic and cleverness. Aset's intervention was not always successful, as shown in one incident where her harpoon missed Sutekh and struck Heru instead.[50] Nevertheless, Heru relied upon his mother's help during other trials, ultimately leading to his victory. The stories in this myth demonstrate how Aset refused to back down when her voice was being silenced and how even in the face of failure, she persevered.

The myths above illustrate several points regarding Aset's agency. She is a Goddess who sought her own power, beyond that which

---

48 Wilkinson (2003), p.148.

49 Papyrus Chester Beatty, 5:2-12; translation from, Kelly Simpson, W. (2003) 'The Contendings of Horus and Seth' (translated by M. Broze). In: Kelly Simpson, W. (ed.) *The Literature of Ancient Egypt: An Anthology of Stories, Instructions, Stelae, Autobiographies, and Poetry* (third edition). London, Yale University Press, pp.91-103.

50 *Papyrus Chester Beatty,* 8:9-10; Kelly Simpson (2003), pp.91-103.

was conferred upon her through marital ties to a powerful God. Not only was she entitled to this sovereignty, but she also earnt it through her own volition. Aset refused to surrender her power to Sutekh when he usurped her crown, just as she repudiated attempts to silence her protests. She never allowed others to belittle and disempower her. In the face of great adversity and trauma, Aset openly expressed her emotions and was not too proud to ask for help when she needed it. Finally, Aset selflessly fought to rescue Wesir and defend Heru, at great personal risk, because she trusted in her power and what she believed in.[51]

The ancient myths of the Goddess Aset can serve as a mythic role model for active agency and taking command of our personal sovereignty. She can teach contemporary spiritual devotees and secular readers alike that we never need to accept another's attempts to disempower us. Furthermore, Aset reassures us that there is no shame in feeling vulnerable at times and that our feelings do not exist at the expense of our strength. The devotion evident in her ancient devotees suggests that they too admired the divine humanity expressed in her mythology. Aset possesses a rich history and mythology, full of magic, love, grief, and wisdom, and her determination is a real source of strength, from which one can draw inspiration today.

---

51 Pinch (2002), p.150.

Reflection of Beauty Shining (Forever)

Elisabeth Slettnes

Daring to Sit in the Red Throne

deTraci Regula

In the early years of my devotion to the Goddess Isis, I was fascinated by the "staircase" on her head. I quickly learned that this was the Throne symbol, and that the Throne of Isis supported, delineated, and held the rulers of Egypt during the long path of Egyptian history. It was a strong symbol of sovereignty, and like the ankh-like tyet or the amulet of Isis, was often considered to be colored red. Some see Isis as merely a personification of the throne, but to me her complex mythology indicates that she was quite a bit more than just a chair imbued with divine energy. She was the female throne, the female seat, the embracer and birther of the pharaoh or of whomever took their place at that seat. This "red throne" has emerged for me at various moments in my journeys to explore ancient sites of Isis.

On one visit to Greece, I encountered an actual "red throne" while visiting the ancient site of Cenchreae where the ruins of the famed temple of Isis described by Apuleius in his "Metamorphoses, or the Golden Ass" stands. There, the throne was a vivid red plastic chair sitting by the submerged outline of the temple, looking out onto the bay. It seemed to be waiting for a goddess – or, I hoped, one of her priestesses – and so I sat down on it and gazed at the water. In Apuleius' novel, the scene at Cenchreae takes place at night when Lucius, despondent at being magically trapped in the form of an ass, pleads for help. A magnificent vision of Isis takes form in front of him, and the Goddess offers him words of comfort and describes how she has arranged that he will lose his asinine form by eating roses carried by one of her priests in the sacred procession that launches the season of navigation.

When I sat down on that red throne, it was not midnight, but midday. In Greece, noon is an equally magical time as the middle of the night. It is considered dangerous to be in the full, sharp sunlight, and it is seen as a time when many spirits are abroad and can do mischief. Even vampires are said to walk at noon in Greece. My experience, fortunately, was different. As I gazed at the water, the sparkling sunlight gleamed so bright that it seemed to wash away my ability to see any colors at all. The water turned grey, the sky turned white, and the obelisk-like shape of the sunbeam on the water directly in front of me looked like moonlight on a night sea. Though it was high midday on a beach in the heart of summer, Isis was transforming the moment into Lucius' midnight vision. Every sparkle seemed to be a word, a hint of the mysteries beyond. I sat frozen in the "red throne" for a long time. When I finally moved, even the bright red chair had for the moment lost its color. I closed my eyes for a time, and finally, when I opened them, the world was back to normal, in full color.

A strong wind came up after I rose from the chair, shaking it and tipping it over. In the stiffening breeze, It seemed amazing that this symbol of the throne had remained perfectly upright on the beach as if waiting for my moment and had not blown away before.

I had another encounter with the experience of sovereignty that the Throne can convey. This was a number of years ago at the Throne Room of the Minoan Palace of Knossos. This divine chair was often described as the "Throne of Minos," the controversial, erratic, womanizing king of ancient Crete. At that time, it was possible to sit for an instant on a replica of the throne nearby in the anteroom. But the replica chair was narrow and rounded, carved in wood after the design of both the ancient stone, one which still stayed in place in the room beyond, and of the charred image of a throne chair that had left its imprint against an interior wall on that spring day long ago when Knossos had burned. Years later, a savvy guide at Knossos would point out that the proportions of the chair were made for a woman, not a man, and he suggested it was made for a queen or a high priestess.

Sitting in this chair gave me several sensations. There was, first of all, the sense of apartness. Only one could be in the chair at a time, and though there was a line of those ready to take my place, for that instant it was indeed mine. But that was not all. There was also the sense of concentration and containment, of restricted movement and because of that, focused attention. One would look ahead at what was in front of the throne. You could not easily escape this. Finally, there was the sense of support. The form of the throne may have restricted me, but it also relaxed my limbs and held me in a posture suitable for meditation and inner attentiveness. All of these traits I find in the energy of Isis as I explore her in personal and direct worship.

I returned to Cenchreae last fall with a group of priestesses. This time, it was late afternoon. There was no red plastic throne chair; only the ruins which had been covered with a tidal flow of water at my first visit were fully visible now. We frolicked on the shore and said our blessings. I did not experience the day-to-night effect again, but instead enjoyed the lively spirit and perhaps something of the festival spirit that Apuleius had described.

While Isis may have acquired the meaning of being the throne, supporting, guarding, and guiding the usually-male occupant, I think the earliest occupant of the Throne would be Isis herself. She is both the throne and the occupant of it. In Egyptian mythology, there is a shared rulership between Isis and Osiris, and then a period of sole rulership by Isis while Osiris goes on his wanderings to inspire and civilize the rest of the world. The most beautiful throne from the tomb of Tutankhamen shows him with his wife Ankesenamun. At many times in ancient Egyptian history, the female line was paramount in establishing a legitimate succession – so a throne without a divine daughter or princess as wife was not enough to assure acceptance. In modern times, we sometimes skip over Isis in her role as supreme and ruling Queen of Egypt, though, surprising to some ears, she survives in Islamic folklore as a wise queen of Egypt.

One of the most simply profound statements on being a priestess of Isis came from a sister priestess, Diveena. She once said in a general conversation that as priestesses, we "must all be our own castle." This was an interesting statement. I asked her about it, and she explained that she meant that we must all have sufficient strength and resources to maintain ourselves. Then we can connect with other individuals, organizations, and movements freely and as equals. I think this remains one of the best explanations of the concept of "sovereignty." We all must be able to reign over our own temples, castles, homes, businesses. If we do it well, it gives us our own independence and power, and allows us to foster that in others. If we need it to be, it can be our own safe, fortified tower, firm against danger or opposition – but in better times, that tower can be the base for a lighthouse which can radiate outwards, illuminating, guiding, and connecting, even with those far away.

Thrones and seats show up in unlikely places, even in ancient geometry. I am fascinated by the discovery of an icosahedron marked with an ancient Egyptian deity on each face. The name "icosahedron" refers to the fifth natural Platonic solid, a twenty-faced shape which was used as a kind of dice in the ancient world. It may have been what was part of the so-called "Alexandrian Game," but the one that intrigues me was found at one of the distant Oases. The word derives from the combination of the Latin word icosa, indicating twenty, and *hedron*, meaning throne or seat. These "thrones" were the "seats" of the chosen divinities, many of which are closely related to the goddess Isis in a number of forms, and to her divine family members of Osiris and Horus.

At our temple here at Isis Oasis Sanctuary in Geyserville, California, we have a number of special throne chairs, including a couple of different replicas of one of the thrones of King Tut. It's interesting to observe how people react to these beautiful chairs – which, after all, are still just chairs, places for people to sit. Some visitors or event participants would clearly never dare to sit on one of them. Others try to organize who is worthy for which chair. But I've also observed hesitant individuals who visibly brace themselves, as if gathering enough power to do so, and then go sit down. If you are open to the energy of what it symbolizes, there can be a tangible influx of energy from these Thrones of Isis. A throne can support, comfort, inspire, connect. I think women who have fully taken their own "throne" are not intimidated by these thrones, and know them for what they are, a tool and a symbol.

Over the years, there has been a lot of criticism of "princesses" and to call someone a "princess" is to indicate a young woman of a rather petulant or difficult type. We have lost the sacred image of the Divine Daughter, produced and beloved by balanced parents, themselves noble kings and noble queens in the truest senses. I think when we sit in the sacred thrones, there is a rekindling of this sense of being the offspring of great beings, and of being a child of the divine, supported, protected, but also presented to the world for service. Perhaps one of our lessons in "sovereignty" is to reclaim the idea of a pure power, harnessed in service, not in oppression.

Goddess Isis

Joey Morris

Soft steps through imprinted sand,
A Journey repeats,
Stepping into the timeless River,
To wash my lashed body,
Cleansing water and fallen tears meet,
I have been broken and
I have been discarded
Torn apart from the inside
Overthrown
I toppled from my own seat,
To taste only dust in my mouth,
Forgetting who I was,
I bathe in my remorse,
And stand at the altar of my foolishness
Naked before you, abrupt in my presence,
Calling out for your blessed wisdom,
I have been parched
And my body concaves into its shell,
Mustering the resilience
To hope again
The water evaporates,
My lips turn to the burning Sun,
Whispering Your name,
Seeking Your balm,
I have been dismembered
By not belonging
A lack of love shadowed my every step,
Left me crumbling,
Yet I remain,
Bathing in Your light,

Memories stretch into view,
Threatening cataclysm,
As you rest Your palm on my brow
Reminding me to partake
Only of my holiness
And where all the cracking joints adjoin
I reunite
With all the wounded parts of myself
I live again
By the breath and grace of She;
Isis.

Great Mother Goddess

Arna Baartz

Illustration from *My Name is Isis* by Susan Morgaine.

The Rulers of Our Own Damn Lives

Monica Rodgers

It was so quick, I would later call the episode a "stress hallucination." In that moment, as my six-year-old daughter clung to my leg silently begging me to protect her from her father's rage, I was shown a line of females from a pyramid, through myself, and ending with my beloved daughter.

While my daughter cleaved, my three-year-old son hid behind the heavy curtains, rocking silently. In the midst of what felt like a hurricane, a great eye of stillness seemed to envelop me, and in it appeared a hologram, streaming forth a firm reminder from some other realm that stated with clarity and conviction: "You are the ruler of your life."

In that moment as I stared down into the pleading eyes of the female child I had birthed, I knew that I would continue the chain of pain and sorrow if I did not break it, right then and there. Although I had never before uttered the words, I declared my decision to get a divorce, and just like that—after almost ten years living in fear and misery—I was free.

The Goddess had just begun her work with me. Following the dissolution of my marriage, I fell deep into a dark night of the soul, becoming bed-ridden as all the misaligned pieces of my life came crashing down around me.

It was in that bed that I descended into to other realms, retrieving pieces of myself from childhood and beyond. I found guides—a medicine woman and a shaman—to help me on my healing journey. Eventually, I began searching for stories of the Goddesses, which would lead me back to the one I had briefly experienced the afternoon my world had begun to change.

Isis visited me through symbols and clues that seemed to intimate my lineage to her. Her name or image would continually show up in Oracle cards, dreams, on jewelry or in books. Each offered me pieces of a larger puzzle that had not fully come into view.

Last summer, I was visiting my childhood home in Maine and felt a deep and desperate urge to drive 45 minutes into Portland to walk the streets by myself. I felt rather silly, but a familiar restlessness seemed to propel me in search of something I could not name.

Eventually I found myself in front of an antique store and felt a giant invisible magnet pulling me inside. I walked directly to a jewelry case in the back, and in that case that had beckoned me, a beautiful small gold Ankh gleamed at me from a black velvet box.

As the woman behind the counter fitted it with a matching chain, she mentioned that she'd never seen such a simple version and that it had just come in the day before. The same day I downloaded the book *Mary Magdalene Revealed* by Meggan Watterson. The same day I'd listened, mesmerized, as she shared her own journey of discovery articulating the link between the suppressed divine feminine and the lineage that led her back to Isis.

Every cell in my body felt on fire.

Shortly after this divinely inspired "coincidence," I had the privilege of working with Sophie Bashford, author of *You are A Goddess* for a channeled reading. During the reading, she guided me through a meditation that led me to Mary Magdalene who, in turn, brought me to the feet of Isis.

The energy I felt coursing through my body as this meditation proceeded was intense. Tears poured down my face as Isis touched my forehead with her finger in the meditation, her image seeming to superimpose upon Mary Magdalene, making me wonder if she was not somehow showing me the reincarnation of her own spirit.

Without words, she told me that I had to forget who I was in order to remember who I was. That we all carry her message inside of us and that we are here to alchemize the spirit (divine) with the matter (human). That we all carry a the divine story within our human bodies.

When women remember *who we truly are*—discarding notions of what we *should* be—we also remember our lineage. We remember Isis and every woman who has come to honor our vow as divine creators. We claim their stories as our own, we gain the mastery to overcome the deeply rooted masculine-feminine imbalance of the patriarchy. We stop giving our power away, and we begin to know that we are the rulers of our own damn lives.

Her Ankh of Sovereignty

Monica Rodgers

Retaining Sovereignty within the Confines of Modern Motherhood

Trista Hendren

Maintaining sovereignty as a mother seems to be an impossible task for many women in capitalist patriarchal societies. I saw a quote on Facebook recently from Mamá Kaur that said, "It's not motherhood that's exhausting. What's exhausting is to nurture in a world that doesn't care for and support its mothers." That rang true for me.

When I was a single mother especially, the last thing I felt was sovereign. As I wrote in *Single Mothers Speak on Patriarchy,* "It's hard to feel like a Goddess when you're worried sick about how you are going to feed your kids. You can do all the affirmations and self-help work you want, but it is a rare woman who feels empowered living in poverty."[52]

Under patriarchy, there is no value in raising children and we are expected to martyr ourselves going at it alone. Glennon Doyle recently wrote, "I burned the memo presenting responsible motherhood as martyrdom. I decided that the call of motherhood is to become a model, not a martyr. I unbecame a mother slowly dying in her children's name and became a responsible mother: one who shows her children how to be fully alive. A broken family is a family in which any member must break herself into pieces to fit in. A whole family is one in which each member can bring her full self to the table knowing that she will always be both held and free."[53] Like many women, I must continue to break the mold that has been handed down for generations in my family. No more broken women. No more broken families.

---

52 For further exploration of single motherhood, see *Single Mothers Speak on Patriarchy*; Girl God Books, 2016.

53 Doyle, Glennon. *Untamed.* Penguin Random House USA, March 2020.

Once I had my 2nd child, I found it impossible to work full-time in the US. The system is set up to fail mothers and children.[54] When my children were young, I had very little help from their father. I soon became a single mother, which left me financially destitute, albeit (mostly) free from his relentless tyranny. Were it not for the help of my mother, I am not sure I would have made it through those years.

Five years ago, I moved with my children to Norway to live with my current husband. Living here has given me a glimpse of some ways women can retain sovereignty in Western cultures with structural support. I will also share what I perceive to be some limitations of the Norwegian system.

I do not believe motherhood was ever meant to be a solitary affair. Being here with my current partner, who does more than his share of the housework, makes me wish I had a different experience when my children were young.

My husband had paternity leave with both of his boys. You can see today the effect this has had on their relationship, even as they have grown into men. This is increasingly common here—and it is mostly paid—split between parents however it works best for their family. In contrast, I did not have any maternity leave after giving birth to my son—and paid into a 6-week (very expensive) insurance plan when I had my daughter.

In Norway, men are expected to be full and equal partners. The first birthday party my 9-year-old daughter attended here caught me completely off guard. The father of her friend was a successful CEO. What was he doing when we returned to pick her up? Vacuuming and (cheerfully) cleaning up after 30 girls! I can't recall *ever* seeing that in the United States.

---

54 I have written more extensively about this in *Single Mothers Speak on Patriarchy* (2016) and *How to Live Well Despite Capitalist Patriarchy* (2019).

A few months later, I had arranged for a play date with another girl for my daughter. The father answered the door. I inquired about the whereabouts of the mother, and was told she was out with friends! He was there taking care of the children and house on his own. Quite frankly, this was so odd to me that I almost did not leave my daughter there. My husband assured me this was quite normal, and after talking with him for a while, I felt at ease.

Today, I often take for granted how much my husband does around the house and with the children. However, I still vividly remember our first parent-teacher conference. My husband went without being asked and fully participated in the hour-long discussion. As we walked out, I started crying. For years, I had only seen other mothers at these meetings at our American schools.

There are also extensive structural support systems in place in Norway. One of which is (almost) free daycare for all from the get-go—as well as generous sick days.

I do not believe that the early childcare is ideal for the overall development of children—although it does free up many things for parents here. Norway also does not have a close extended family network. That said, I think Scandinavia is about as good as it gets for parents in the Western world.

I would also like to point to my (adopted) family in Lebanon as another way forward. I believe the village community-based parenting would have really benefited all of us when my kids were young. The children belong to everyone. Families get together for extended late lunches where they share cooking tasks. I suppose it depends on the family, but I have never experienced a family anywhere were there is more support, joy and sense of belonging —despite Lebanon's decades of war and economic hardship.[55]

---

55 I divorced my first husband in 2000, but I still stay in contact with most of the family, including my ex, who remains one of my dearest friends.

That said, there is almost no structural support in Lebanon for mothers, so if you marry into the wrong family, things can be quite disastrous. My friend Nohad Nassif wrote a brilliant book addressing this.[56] She believes Universal Basic Income is the answer to this—and I agree with her. Sovereignty in motherhood should include all women.

That said, I wonder what going further back can teach us.

Leslene della-Madre reminds us that, "Isis veneration spread as far east as Afghanistan, to the Black Sea, as well as to what is now western Europe in Portugal and as far north as England. It is Her legacy that has been inherited by christianity as revealed in the icons of the Black Madonnas found all over Europe; Isis and Her son Horus suckling at Her breast are most likely the prototypes for Mary and Jesus."[57]

So what is the psychological impact over the last 2,000 years of changing the once-sovereign images of Isis suckling Horus to passive images of Mary with Jesus? As someone who breastfed my children for over four years, I can attest that this is a holy and sacred act. I still look in reverence when I see a woman breastfeeding her baby. But it also takes a lot out of you. I have never been so thin (or exhausted) as in my post-breastfeeding years. And we don't live in a world that helps mothers rest and recover.

Mary Condren wrote, "We now have enough evidence to suggest that there have been radical consequences for women when the dominant cultural symbol systems are exclusively male, or feature women whose identity is entirely derivative or serving a patriarchal status quo, i.e., many representations of the Virgin Mary. The absence of empowering female images both reflects

---

56 Nassif, Nohad. *ARAB humanist: The Necessity of Basic Income*. Noon & Ta, LLC; January 2019.

57 Della-Madre, Leslene. "The Luminous Dark Mother"

and affects the subordination of women. This very lack shapes and deforms the way our drives are constructed so that both body and soul are put in the service of the patriarchal social order."[58]

Growing up in the church, I learned that my role in life was to be subservient to men. I saw my mother abide by all the rules. (Until she didn't.) What would my mother's experience have been if Isis/Auset were her archetype instead of the Catholic Mary she grew up with? Could she have attained sovereignty earlier in her life?

In contrast, Isis is said to have appeared at the sanctuary of Isis at Philae and said, "I am Nature, the universal Mother, mistress of all the elements, primordial child of time, sovereign of all things spiritual, queen of the dead, queen also of the immortals, the single manifestation of all gods and goddesses that are."[59]

In a paper by Marianna Delray discussing Isis and Mary, she explains, "Isis was worshipped as the saviour goddess, and it was believed that her divine milk gave protection and reviving power... Isis was accredited with numerous powers and even in later times she continued to be the goddess of immense importance in Egypt and beyond. Indeed, following Hellenisation, the cult of Isis spread throughout the Mediterranean, assimilating into the cults of other Mediterranean nursing deities... Lucius describes Isis as 'holy and eternal saviouress of the human race, ever beneficent in cherishing mortals, who indeed bestowed the sweet affection of a mother upon the tribulations of the unfortunate.' In the Metamorphoses, Isis speaks about herself as the 'mother of the entire universe, mistress of all the elements and remarks that

---

58 Condren, Mary. "On Forgetting Our Divine Origins: The Warning of Dervogilla." *Irish Journal of Feminist Studies* vol. 2 no. 1 (1997): 117-132.
59 Birnbaum, Lucia Chiavola Ph.D. "African Dark Mother - Oldest Divinity We Know." Authors Choice Press, 2001.

while she is one 'divinity,' she is worshipped by 'ten thousand names' throughout the world."[60]

This sounds very different from what we know about Mother Mary. For those of us who grew up in the church, the idea of a savior GODDESS is quite a remarkable thealogy to behold.

Rev. Dr. Karen Tate wrote, "We're allowed to have the Great Mother in our spiritual paradigm if she is docile and tame like Mary, or as the Goddess that saves women in childbirth or men from bombs and typhoons. But would patriarchy have us reclaim the full meaning of the Queen Mother of Compassion, or any Goddess, if it meant that embodying her might bring our world into balance and emulating her caused women to no longer serve the status quo?"[61]

Modern motherhood really needs to move beyond the status quo. There are very few places on earth that really provide a foundation where it works *well*—for women *and* children. In the interim, building our own 'villages' with like-minded sister-friends may provide better support.[62]

My children are teenagers now, so my mothering is much less time-consuming. It mostly consists of being present for them and guiding them to make good choices for their futures. I have tried to raise my children as sovereign beings since they were very small. While this was challenging at times, I am reaping the benefits now via a trusting and open relationship with my kids and their friends. My hope is that in reclaiming my own sovereignty, I will teach them to do the same.

---

60 Delray, Marianna. "Legacy of the Egyptian Goddess? A Retrospective Look at the Two Divine Mothers, Isis and Mary." Macquarie University; 2017. Accessed on Academia.com

61 Tate, Karen Rev. Dr. *Goddess Calling: Inspirational Messages & Meditations of Sacred Feminine Liberation Thealogy.* Changemakers Books; March 2014.

62 Further discussions of this can be found in *How to Live Well Despite Capitalist Patriarchy* and *Single Mothers Speak on Patriarchy.*

Isis Mothers the World

Arna Baartz

Illustration from *My Name is Isis* by Susan Morgaine.

Dedication to Isis

Carmel Glenane

In my heart, The Mother Isis lives.
In my heart, The Mother Isis listens.
She hears my aching heart, and it is her heart that aches too.

Isis, my Mother, listen to my call for help,
I am afraid, dear Mother.

I hear you my child, you are forever in my heart,
as I wash your wounds in love.
I know love. I am love, and I bring to you now "the call",
My call, for you to awaken from your fear of love, to embrace "Me."

Come my child; come, come, come unto me,
I am "She", and "She" is me.
All life comes from me, All life moves through me, All life is released through me.

In my arms you now sleep, In my arms you now heal, In my arms you find love.

I am with you till the end of time, as I am the end of time. Breathe me now into your heart,
Forgive Every Living Thing,
And you too, can be with me.

~Carmel Glenane ©2015

Finding the Goddess in Lebanon

Christine Shahin

The year 2012 was the start of a deep metamorphic experience for me. I overcame a large number of deaths in my immediate and extended family, my small niche business was growing with all the transitional pains that are part of any birthing process, and I was running for County Legislature, while embracing a milestone birthday. As a result of this grieving period, my children had created an online birthday gift appeal from family and friends to send me to Lebanon, the land of my family's stories.

The excitement of this gift was eclipsed by the hard emotional space of my heart, so my journey to Lebanon happened the following year, where I was joined with my two daughters, Lena and Shadia. My cousin Barbara, her husband Mahmoud, and their son Jad, then a senior in high school, received us.

My children had already been to Lebanon before I was ever able to, so this was a return for them. Thankfully, Shadia was taking Arabic classes so she was able to bridge my language gap.
My closest girlfriend Emmy, who passed in 2012, had always encouraged me to go to Lebanon after her trip to Italy, the country of her ancestors, saying "there's just something about seeing whole towns where people look like you." While there was some of that recognition in Lebanon, Beirut was so racially and culturally diverse, that I was told I did not look Lebanese at all by some.

My daughters and I traversed from the Corniche Boardwalk in Beirut, where people fished the Mediterranean Sea in cutoff jeans under plush, high-rise buildings, to the mountains of Jazien; from the Souq of Saida to the Ehden Nature Preserve; from the Jeita Grotto, home of the world's largest known stalactite, to the Chouf in Bsharri, home of Khalil Gibran; and the Qadisha

Valley with the #1 Taxi Driver/Guide Michel, who took us home for lunch with his beautiful wife and children.

It was in Jbeil/Byblos as we were walking through the ancient ruins that we almost missed one of the most profound, underground ancient remains of our trip. There was a small, unassuming marker standing alone as we turned the grassy bend. It looked as though there was nothing to see, but still I stopped to read it. "This is the site of the original source well of the goddess Isis," it stated.

Lena & Shadia

The unnoticeable marking then elaborated on how devotees would gather at designated times to worship and receive the abundant water of the well, now dry. Stories of the goddess Isis are usually attributed to ancient Egypt, but here was an original well of water in her name in Lebanon.

Excited, I walked towards the nothingness, discovered an edge, and peered down to find this breathtaking site. I removed my sandals so I could scamper down the worn staircase to the well, my daughters following behind. The well is built deep, with ancient stones serving dual purpose as wall and steps that lead to the actual stone wellhead.

The goddess Isis is most known for the deep grief she feels after losing her love Osiris and rising above the pain to a new power. Depending on who is telling the story, her love is either her son or her brother, which, seen through patrilineal sight, is taken literally and is seen as immoral. Matrilineal sight, on the other hand, sees all people as children of mother or as siblings, which would make my husband, though his genealogy is European, my (spiritual) brother, and a son of a mother.

When the goddess Isis set out to find the dead body of her love, the search took her to Phoenicia, where she met Queen Astarte, who hired the goddess Isis as a nursemaid to her infant prince as she didn't recognize her as the goddess.

Isis grew fond of Astarte's son and decided to make him immortal. Astarte entered as Isis was holding the royal child over the ritual fire. Assuming her son was being harmed, Queen Astarte instinctively grabbed her son from the flames, thereby undoing the rite of Isis that would have made the boy a god.

Isis then affirmed her identity and shared her quest to recover her husband's body. As Astarte listened, she realized that the body was hidden in the center of the palace and told Isis in which fragrant tree it was.

After securing her love Osiris' body, Isis then hid it in the swamps of the River Nile, waiting to carry his remains back to Egypt for a proper burial. The box containing Osiris' body was discovered by Set, his murderer, while out hunting. Enraged, Set hacked Osiris' body into 14 pieces and threw them far and wide in different directions, believing that crocodiles would eat them.

After endlessly searching once again for her lost love, Isis found Osiris' body parts and rejoined them, bringing her husband back to life. Together, they conceived a child, Horus, who later became the Sun God. Osiris, now assured that Horus would sooth Isis' grief, descended to become the King of the Underworld, ruling over the dead and the sleeping, though his spirit frequently returned to be with his beloved wife and son, who remained under his watchful and loving eye.

There are many deviations of this story. In some, Isis found the body of Osiris in Byblos; in another the goddess eats the dismembered parts of her husband and brings him back to life as her son Horus. In another account, Isis morphs into a sparrow hawk fluttering over Osiris, fanning life back into him with her long wings.

The common thread in these differing versions is the resurrection of life over death and the transcendent feminine ability to create new life from profound grief.

The discovery of this wellhead brought me back to my own purpose in life. It was 2006 when I decided to become an entrepreneur, creating my all-natural wellness beauty consulting business, now a full service natural salon/spa. I wanted to name it after a goddess, as they are often associated with beauty and love, and I wanted her to come from the land of my roots. I chose Astarte, unbeknownst of her relationship to Isis, but because she is considered Phoenician.

A framed papyrus image of the ancient Egyptian goddess Isis hangs in my salon/spa and reminds me of the many timeless gifts she has given all women: the embodiment of determination; the capacity to feel and grieve deeply and to rise anew; the source of sustenance and protection; the discerning power of passion and compassion, rather than logic or brute strength; and the ability to use personal gifts to create what we want, rather than living in constant reaction to what we don't want.

That renewal of body is important and love is a feeling that is not static, but a force for action that can conquer death, creating a new way of living. It was this journey to Lebanon and reuniting with family – some I met for the first time – that began my inner journey of self-healing and brought me to the world of ancient feminine wisdom found at the well.

Isis Mask

Lauren Raine

From the *Masks of the Goddess Project*, which ran from 1998-2019.

The Importance of The Correct Name

Tyreesha Garrett

It is critical to learn the origins of Auset (a Goddess of Kemet, commonly known as ancient Egypt) in African history. In the time of European invasion/colonization of Kemet, there were many violent acts by Europeans that took place against Kemet. One being plagiarism (theft), of Kemet's legacy, in which Auset's name and image was taken by Europeans. Europeans wrongfully claimed and changed her name to Isis as a representation of European legacy. Knowing and calling Auset by only the name Isis continues to perpetuate the lie of a legacy that has been stolen. The attack on Africa's legacy has been happening for centuries. When considering Isis, it is crucial that the truth of her original name and existence is represented, as this also reflects the legacy and the people she originated from. This ties into African people's (i.e., African Americans) images. If you take away a people's true history and replace it with an inhumane history (i.e., the history of enslavement) this will impact how they view themselves. It is an intentional robbing of their cultural identity. In this case, knowing the truth will significantly impact how young girls/women of African descent view and value themselves. We can start to cultivate our true value in who we are in our greatness.

Racism is so embedded in our society and it systemically plays a role in how little girls and women of African descent view themselves. We are so bombarded by information that tells us that we are less than (inferior), not good enough and we have no idea this is a complete lie. Some of us must wait until we become older to learn (whether self-education or another way) that we were told lies and find our true worth, which leads to confidence. It is important for us to learn and know our own true history beyond the (Atlantic Slave Trade) which is commonly taught to us in the public school system, so that we can now begin to restore our true worth.

If our focus is to encourage and support the truth of all young girls' and women's images, this also includes young girls and women of African descent.

Isis as a Woman of Color

Susan Morgaine

Go to your favorite search engine and type "Goddess Isis" into images. What common denominator do you see? I will give you a minute.

Most of these depictions of Isis show Her as a white woman. It is the same as Hollywood depicting Cleopatra, a Priestess of Isis, as a white woman, as portrayed by Elizabeth Taylor in 1963.

The similarities are striking. Cleopatra, of course, was Greek, and so her appearance as a white woman may not be as detrimental as showing Isis the Goddess as a white woman.

Isis is seen as an Egyptian Goddess, but She was first known as Auset/Aset and originated in Nubia, an ancient region in Northeast Africa, also known as Kush. She was worshiped by the Kushites in Nubia as far back as 1950 BCE, and was known to them as the great lady of Nubia.

Worship of Auset grew far and wide, from Nubia to Egypt, the country with which She is most associated. But from there, Her worship traveled to Greece and Rome, where it was then brought to the British Isles. It was in Greece that Her name was forever changed to Isis.

No matter where Her worship spread, however, people depicted Her as they saw themselves, similar to how Jesus is depicted as a white man with blue eyes.

However, whether Isis is originally from Nubia or Egypt, the fact remains that She is not now, nor ever was, a white woman. She is a powerful, beautiful woman of color. This needs to be reclaimed, not in his-story, but in her-story.

In this time of Black Lives Matter, where white people are (hopefully) starting to see the injustices and inequality inherent in the systemic racism around the world, it becomes even more important to point out that the Goddess Auset, now known as Isis, is a woman of color. (Note: I am not a woman of color, although my DNA shows that I have 10% African ancestry, of which I am proud.)

It is important that women everywhere, but especially women of color, reclaim Auset as their own and depictions of her need to stop being "white-washed," as so much else in history has been. We need to see Her depicted more as She was in life than in the imagination of white people.

Re-Membering Our Sovereign Divinity

Duann Kier

My path to sovereignty is still in process as a 65-year-old crone, and the journey to this time in my life has been with much bumbling and stumbling. It is one of the lesser known stories of Isis that speaks to me most deeply.

The story begins with the acknowledgment that Ra, the great grandfather of Isis, was an old god. Let me explain.

My mother was a Christian fundamentalist and my father almost an atheist. Their codependent relationship made for quite a battleground in our home, and I decided at a very early age that I would never get married or have any children. I had witnessed my mother's submissive fear that she might not be able to make it on her own financially with a child in tow. She stayed in a state of perpetual anxiety that my father might leave or die and leave her in abject poverty.

Even though my mother was known as the best cook in the family, I consciously chose not to learn how to do so. And I had absolutely no desire to babysit children of any age when I was in high school, especially infants. They were too needy and dependent upon others for their survival. They could make you dependent upon a man for your own.

My mother's only source of comfort seemed to be the church. She would take me with her and we would come home to a man in a foul mood with a distasteful look on his face. She would rush to fix lunch and then the rest of the day would be spent in a holy hell of yelling and screaming or stone, cold silence. Soon it was too much for her, so she began to drop me off at church and pick me back up afterward. Then I began to go on my own.

She continued to hold out hope that my father would become a Christian and value her the same way that Jesus supposedly valued his own bride, the church. I held out hope that one day I would be able to save her from it all and spent much of my life trying to do so. Ahh! The burdens of daughters toward their mothers when their mothers are unable or unwilling to save themselves.

My times at church seemed to give me a reprieve from all the tension at home and I began to see it as the family for which I achingly longed. And the story of Jesus coming back at some pie-in-the-sky future spoke to my very soul. *I recognized it.* How? At an early age, I would stand at my bedroom window and state that I was ready to go back home—that I could not be in this family, on this planet. Things did not work here the way they did back home and they needed to come back and get me. After hearing the stories of Jesus when I was a child, I thought, "Oh, that's who it must be! He and his angels are the ones coming back to get me!" I now know different, but that is a story for another time.

Because of my psychic ability, I had been seeing visions and hearing voices almost since the day I was born. My mother had, too, but she was afraid they were demonic or satanic. And, of course, it was also her fear of how my father would react. I was well into my adulthood before I found out that he could occasionally see dead people and that he only went to the local poker game on Friday night when he had gotten the message that he was going to win. His Scandinavian father could hear long distance conversations and was obsessed with the work of Edgar Cayce on Atlantis. And there was also his grandfather who had been a cattle whisperer and his Irish mother's brother who had been a water witch, someone who could find water on your property with a stick.

I now wonder if my parents made some sort of soul contract to bring me into the world so I would inherit the gifts in their family lines. My ancestors go back to the ancient Creek and Mayans and even the Gypsies. But for the purposes of this essay, it may be even more providential that I carry within me the DNA of Tjuye, a high priestess of the Goddess Hathor. She was the mother of Queen Tiye and the grandmother of Akhenaten.

It was not just the story of Jesus that spoke to me. There were biblical stories of angels and dreams and numerology and astrology and divination and automatic writing and seers and talking animals and resurrections from the dead. My middle name Duann is after my father Duane, but my first name Deborah is after the first woman judge of Israel in the Old Testament. Believe it or not, she was actually a prophetess of the Goddess Asherah, but again, that is another story.

Just as I questioned the inequalities in my own blood family, I could not help but question the inequalities in my new-found spiritual one. I woke up to the fact that I was following a male god without a female Goddess and that he had only one son and no daughters. His followers insisted that his son had never married and had even been celibate his whole life. This god's book was written by only men about his most important male followers and the most important male followers of his son. The preachers in his pulpits and the deacons on his boards were all male. Women were hardly ever mentioned except in submissive, subservient roles—just like my mother had been.

CLICK! Was there a connection between my mother's subservient role to my father and the subservient role of all women in her/our religion? If so, would it not be true about all the other religions based on a male-only god?

I had been told that Jesus came to show us that this god was actually a loving father, but for some reason, he was still blood-thirsty enough to need a human (or divine?) sacrifice to save us from the hell he had created for us just in case we didn't love him back. It became blatantly obvious to me that my loving spiritual family was banded together not in love, but in fear, and that their paranoia was leading most of them to be sexist, racist and homophobic. This time the fear in my family was not based on my mother's anxiety about being left in abject poverty. This time the fear in my family was caused by hellfire and brimstone. And to add insult to injury, it was all Eve's fault.

So, let me follow in the footsteps of my no longer needed savior, Jesus, and speak to you in parables. This parable is not the very likely male-washed version of the one we find today of the story of Isis and Ra:

Ra was an old god. He was so old that he had begun to drool, but he refused to give up the reins to the sun chariot he flew across the sky every day. He wanted everyone to continue to see him in all his blazing glory. At night, he became a frightened little boy as he descended into the darkness of the underworld to fight his demons.

Ra had come forth from his mother, Nun, but everyone, especially himself, had forgotten about her and believed he had given birth to himself. He even believed he alone had given birth to his children. He needed no Goddess as his mother nor did he need a Goddess as the mother of his children.

As Ra grew feebler, he became jealous of his great granddaughter, the Goddess Isis, and her serpent of ancient wisdom and healing. She had magical powers he did not possess and he feared that one day he would be dependent upon her magical gifts of healing and resurrection.

After a long night of fighting his demons in the darkness of the underworld, Ra fell deathly ill on his sun chariot one morning as he tried to rise into the sky. He screamed out in pain for his mother. All the gods heard his anguished cries and rushed to offer their recommendations, but none of the well-discussed proposals eased Ra's suffering. They hesitated to call on a Goddess for help, but finally sent out the clarion call for Isis.

Isis spread her wings and rushed to the aid of her great grandfather. She wiped the drool from his mouth and held his trembling body in her arms, rocking him to and fro as she sang her song of healing. The vibrations of her voice found their way to the deep source of his pain—his own inner demons—and the god began to breathe easier and fell fast asleep in her lap. He dreamed of his mother and the songs she had sung to him as a child. And he cried in remembrance of her. The gods gathered round in reverence and awe at the magic Isis possessed. The Goddesses simply smiled in their knowing.

When Ra awoke in his chambers, he bolted to his sun chariot and rose into the sky for all to see him once again in his fully blazing glory. He knew he was a sight to see as he set the whole sky on fire. And then he heard the chorus of the people.

Praise be to Isis, the Goddess of a Thousand Names!
Greater than the names of all the gods and Goddesses is her name!
She sets the sun in the sky and has the power over life and death!
Praise be to Isis, the Mother of Us All!

Ra boiled himself into a rage. Her name was now greater than his? Had she not lowered herself to wipe the very drool from his mouth? He called together his male-only Council of Gods.

"As you can see," he said, "my great granddaughter Isis was able to heal me from my terrible affliction. Have you asked yourselves why?"

The gods mumbled among themselves in deliberation, much as they had done when Ra had fallen ill, but once again, they remained perplexed.

"It's because she's the one who made me ill!" exclaimed Ra. "She used my bodily fluids to create that serpent of hers and it attacked me in the underworld! Then she used it to heal me! She never would have been able to do this if she hadn't stolen the power from me to begin with!"

Well, that certainly made sense, all the gods agreed, forgetting that they were the ones who had called upon the Goddess Isis because she had always had the gift of healing and they were unable to render such aid to their highest god. Isis must be punished!

Ra summoned the god Set to his side.

"Set, my great grandson and the brother of Isis will deliver our judgement," Ra proclaimed. "He has proven himself faithful during our battles together in the underworld."

Turning to Set, the old god declared, "Go kill your brother Osiris, for he is the heart of Isis. This will put her in her place and keep her there, submissive in her grief."

Most of us know the rest of the more traditional story of Isis and Osiris—how their brother Set dis-membered Osiris and disseminated his pieces throughout Egypt and how their sister Nephthys helped Isis find the pieces for Isis to re-member them and resurrect Osiris. We may not, however, be as familiar with how this played out in "reality" in more modern-day Egypt.

The Temple of Isis near Aswan was originally located on the high rocky island of Philae in the middle of the Nile in Southern Egypt. During the reign of the Eastern Roman Emperor Justinian, the temple was converted into a Christian church and all the "pagan" artifacts were defaced. Later, with the completion of the Aswan Lower Dam project in 1899, the Nile began periodically flooding the temple. Before completing the Aswan High Dam in 1970, the main temple complex was dis-membered and re-membered once again on the even higher island of Agilika, just northwest of Philae.

In essence, the Temple of Isis was resurrected from its watery depth in the underworld.

And this is where I find my own sovereignty—going deep into the emotional depths of my own underworld and coming to terms with myself to make different choices than my mother and the women before me.

In my story, Isis gives away her healing magic to a god who not only does not appreciate her service, but actually resents her gifts. She finally rebels when he goes for her heart. Through the loving wings of Isis, I have learned to rebel and not serve a similar god, no matter what religion he represents.

After Set dis-members the man she loves, Isis resurrects Osiris by helping him re-member his scattered pieces, but he still must descend into the underworld. Through the loving wings of Isis, I have learned I can hold sacred space for the men I love if they are willing to work toward wholeness, but it is not my responsibility to do their emotional work for them.

Nephthys, the sister of Isis, wept uncontrollably with her over the death and dismemberment of their brother Osiris by their brother Set. Through the loving wings of Isis, I have learned that it is my sisters who will sit and weep with me when I am grieving loss, whether that be of someone I love or the loss of myself in the processing of loving someone. And as sisters, we can mourn the violence that men inflict upon men, and women as well, because they have not descended deep enough into their own emotional underworld to face the darkness inside them and around them. It is a job that all of us must do for ourselves, but it seems women are more willing to do their emotional work because of their familiarity with the darkness of the womb from which all new life springs.

The priestesses at the Temple of Philae must have mourned deeply the loss of their beloved Goddess Isis to the encroaching Christian religion. And I am sure it was especially disheartening to watch as the church usurped the statues of Isis holding her infant Horus and perverted them into Mary holding the infant Jesus.

Through the loving wings of Isis, I now know she is resurrecting those same priestesses today, just as she resurrected the temple in which they served her. And she calls not for our worship of her, but our embodiment of her. The days of worship are over. The old gods do not deserve it, and as the embodiments of the Goddess herself, we no longer bow to anyone.

Isis as Kite

Hayley Arrington

Tea Leaves

Jessica Morell

That which dropped her to her knees
Those, oh – were the years
That chaos & dark longing towards
What
She could not have named
There were those hours when
With
Crazed wings
She flew against the cage formed around her guarded heart
A cage constructed to hide the
Shame
Of a shattered heart
Those pieces, seemingly irreparable,
Too many, to ever fit back together
Into
Any semblance of order.
And yet – despite dire predictions,
Hour after hour
With
Great and terrible deliberation
It was constructed
And in & through that repair
A great chest/a treasure chest of a human chest/ribs sore from such a
Beating,
From the inside, no less.
Viscera exposed
A great throbbing,
Beating, that now anyone could hear. The most
Common
Of things.
This beating & pumping of great

Volumes
Of blood
Plasma, that poured bidden, wide & viscous,
All could see and there was no
Shame.
A women's blood
Pouring
From a heart/pouring from a
Secret.
In ancient days was known to hold great power,
Revered
Caught in sacred jugs.
Used for fertility rites, known to
Potentiate
Even the weakest cause.
From within, she knew/one day/fully/ as it were
Atavistic
Knowledge, rather than just learned.
That, being put back together was a much finer thing than being left
Whole.
Untested, Untempered.
And in this, she turned away from the cold comfort – meaning no comfort at all – from the teat of pain upon which she had suckled.
She demanded milk for all that blood – explained the tenants of a fair
Bargain and began the remarkable task of learning to
Nourish herself on
Honey and tea leaves.

Bowl

Jessica Morell

Bowled over – vessel
Vein, half-full, filled, physical –
Open palms, open to you –
Whisper, wonder, wish
Mull, Mule, Milk
Fluid, falling by drops from my breast
And you,
A beast.
Who came
To lap at the pool of my being –
Viscous/felt like oil
Like broth
Like semen
Like tears
And, like all good witches,
she emptied herself completely,
so that she might be filled/full of spirit – of voice/of
wind/light/wax – melted liquid, taking form into a new shape:
Hair wild, eyes bright, teeth show between parted lips – her beau-
ty flashing between expressions of anguish/joy/rhythm/entitle-
ment
Heat/hot/hidden/house – hope/hope not/hope to/hopeful
Help – reach out/she does/left palm open to caress, most tenderly, your sweet face
Right Hand/tight, an open fist – she
contradicts/rages/wounds/soothes and betrays
Changes –
fierce to sullen
sullen to sad
and sad
to

passion and grace
her voice/ a song/ a sound/ a harp and a harpy too
Wicked and wonderful – her love boundless/ a sea/ a tsunami
A doll's toy/ a bowl for a tiny bit of a creature/ a crumb/ a crack/ a falling – wild free fall into that fissure
And emerging somewhere else – a different time and place
And yet, still that terrible unknowing/knowing of yearning
Same spirit contained in someone else's body – same hell bent glow of fire
Fine as porcelain/burnt brittle but better
Hand painted – how could any one have known that priceless drawing by some ancient hand was covering something even older/ atavistic visage/ what price did she pay to be so adorned?
Burn away that and see what's below/the bones/the frame – the story waiting to be unearthed/excavated/peel back the centuries/the hours
Uncover/display/discover
Desire to taste
Touch, feel, hold – this life
The one, like Alice, she fell into/down/down
A crevice, a rabbit hole, a hillside
A falling into
The sky
The moon
The sea

Everything known but nothing remembered...
Finding herself/finding her other/her doppelganger
A mirror image/ a lover/ a sister/ a memory
A path
No return,
On the spiral path
No return.

Finding Isis: My Journey Toward Sovereignty

Arlene Bailey

What is it about Isis that draws so many to her? Why after thousands of years does she still create a mystery of awe and power that spins this cocoon around us, holding us as we grow and transform? Just like a Mother with a child.

When I first discovered the world of Goddesses and nature-based spiritual traditions, one of the first questions I was always asked is *what pantheon do you follow... which Goddess do you serve?* This was almost invariably followed by *I serve Isis*. After hearing this same response from almost every woman I encountered, I actually developed a distaste for all things Egyptian and especially Isis. I still didn't have a particular pantheon but, being one who did not like following the herd, I knew I didn't want to be one more devotee of Isis.

Over the years I finally discovered that alignment for me was alignment with my ancestral roots which were Celtic. I still did not *serve* a particular Goddess for the idea of *serving* felt too much like aspects of the religion I'd fought so hard to leave. It would take me many years and, much inner work traveling through various traditions and ideas, to be able to separate enough from the trappings of the religious indoctrination of my youth to find an opening to what worked best for me.

My first actual experience with Isis came during one of my first Shamanic Journeys. As with all Journeys there was much there, but what I remember – what to this date (almost 20 years later) is still so very vivid – is the image of me being carried in a litter, like a queen, by four men who were dressed in the Egyptian style of ancient Egypt. This carriage of sorts was extremely ornate and deeply *what I called then* cobalt blue with gold. I would later realize it was the blue of lapis lazuli. I remember the visual being very much an out of body experience as I looked upon the queen who looked like me. I remember thinking *why am I in this thing and dressed this way?* Then I saw her... a woman standing off to the side... a woman looking at me... a woman who, well, looked like the pictures of Isis I'd seen. A woman who *was* Isis. Then she spoke and said *you dismiss me, eschew me and possibly even hate who and what I stand for. But remember. You were me and I am you.* Then everything vanished and I came out of the Journey.

I remember thinking *why Isis*??? *Why me?* Though visibly shaken, I still had no connection to or resonance with her and could not understand why, of all people, she would come to me in this way. So I left it all there thinking it was an isolated experience and that was that.

Over the next seven or so years, every now and then Isis would pop into my consciousness in one way or the other, but I still felt no real connection. Actually, I think I refused to feel a connection because I didn't want to be the same as everyone else. Isis was still the main Goddess/Deity most people I met aligned with and I still fought being the same.

In 2014, I decided to do some personal work with a sister Priestess skilled in Shamanic Breathwork.™ We did several Breathworks over the 5-day intensive, but there is one, like that experience with the Shamanic Journey, that even today still gives me chills. As I went into the breath I found myself dancing on top of an emerald green knoll overlooking the ocean in Ireland. It was not unusual for me to begin Journeys or Breathworks this way, always dancing and my red hair flying. Suddenly I looked to the far right of me and realized the Veil had thinned and I could see to the other side. I stopped moving and watched as a woman came through the Veil directly toward me. It was Isis in all her lapis and gold glory walking straight toward me very deliberately and with a huge smile on her face. Slowly she began to morph into another woman and I remember my breath becoming very erratic and tears flowed down my face as Isis became my Mother. Both with dark hair and dark features, but the woman who now stood before me was not Isis who had crossed the Veil, but my *actual* mother who, at that time, had been dead for 36 years. She embraced me and held me and then faded back into the mist.

It took a long time to process this experience and even today I get weak and weepy. In my mind's eye it was so real... is still so eerily real and as though it happened yesterday and in this time and reality. I could never completely understand why both Isis and my Mother were one and the same and yet separate and different. Then it came to me... Isis *was* my mother, both my actual mother and The Great Mother of all that ever has been and ever will be. That experience completely changed me and allowed an opening for Isis to become part of my life. I still did not *serve* or *worship* her nor take on the Egyptian pantheon, but my heart was able to open and let her in. My roots are Celtic – Nordic even – and Ireland and Scotland and that lineage and mythology was what felt like home to me. I had, however, found a way to at least not dismiss Isis or her lineage just because I didn't want to be like everyone else. I finally realized I could have my own relationship with this Great Mother. I thought that was enough and all the first Shamanic Journey and this Shamanic Breathwork™ was meant to be.

Until another Breathwork a year or so later...

I remember riding the breath and immediately being back on that grassy knoll, dancing and hair flying but this time in the blue robes of a Priestess. Then I was being dragged aboard a ship and sailing for many days away from my home. I don't remember many other scenes until the one where I was in a throne room... sitting on the throne... still in blue robes, but instead of the robes of a Priestess, I wore the robes of a Queen.

Suddenly I was back on that grassy knoll again, dancing with red hair flying. Once again the Veil thinned and both my Mother and Isis walked toward me, side by side, holding hands, smiling. This time there were two women, not one morphing into the other. I smiled too and opened my arms to welcome these Mothers, but right before they got to me they faded back into the mist but not before offering a potent reminder... *Remember Your Mother, Remember The Great Mother.*

It was at that moment that I came out of the Breathwork. I cried for days, longing, remembering, smiling. Once again it would take months, years even, to sort it all out.

In the meantime, little isolated things gently introduced me to a deeper place within the Egyptian pantheon.

First came Bast.

Then Sekhmet.

Then once again Isis, but not in a Journey or a Breathwork, but on my canvas, first as *The Queen of Herself* and then again as the *Great Cosmic Mother.*[63]

Even so, I still had trouble connecting it all. Memories flowed in and out until one day I remember smiling for it felt like all the dots, all the different messages and images had finally created a whole.

---

63 You can see *Great Cosmic Mother* on page 115 and *Queen of Herself* on page 30.

Me. ME!

I was the Whole.

Just as with Osiris, Isis had put ME back together.

It took many years across this and other lifetimes, but this Great Mother kept calling her daughter home.

All those years...

And...

Until today I thought this was the end of the story. However, I recently created another painting that was to be a cave wall similar to those of ancient times. It turned out differently however, with the strangest collection of things demanding to be part of the whole. One day as I sat looking at the canvas, this cave wall of my lifetimes, it suddenly hit me. Oh holy wow, now I understood why the pyramids, Sekhmet as a lion and the Tower on the Tor showed up as they did... why there was such insistence that a small Ankh be placed in the section called *The Dreamtime*. I had never connected the dots until now, seeing that juxtaposition of things as just strange rather than connected. Going back to that final Breathwork it all makes sense now. To do a painting of my lives within lives would never have been complete without the Avalon/Egypt connection that showed up in that last Breathwork. Had I remembered that, well, things would have been different. I can only guess I wasn't meant to have that piece of the puzzle until now.

Even though I was never actually looking, I've spent many years *Finding Isis* and I feel this will continue to happen as I move toward that one last piece... pieces... this Great Mother, as

Goddess of Crone Mysteries and Life and Death, continues to hold for me.

Holy Wow.

All those times I wasn't looking and still She, Isis... Auset Isis... found me.

Duwa Auset, Duwa[64]

---

64 *Duwa Auset, Duwa –Thou are Goddess the most High (Khemetic)*

Great Cosmic Mother

Arlene Bailey

Memphis: A Day Off From School

Sharon Putnam

In 1977, my parents took our family to New Orleans Museum of Art to see the "Treasures of Tutankhamun" exhibit. This was my first introduction to Isis. As awesome as the golden burial mask is to most, seeing the Isis wings and the role she and other women held in society and Egyptians' beliefs impacted me and stuck with me.

Isis (along with other goddesses) was present on the tomb walls, on the outside of a golden shrine holding the pharaoh's canopic chest and jars, on one of the pharaoh's coffins, on symbolic jewelry, and among other items found in his tomb. Isis' outstretched wings captured my interest.

That women could be rulers, pharaohs, and divinity also captured my interest. Names such as Nefertiti, Hatshepsut, and Cleopatra evoke images of powerful women reigning on earth, but Isis reigned in the heavens and over things on earth.

If she was this important and powerful, it meant that I, too, could be. I could see myself as divine, belonging to this world as I am. A golden spark of divinity in each of us as we are. In knowing these things, She, Isis, helped me on my path.

I Can Hear Her Breathing

Rev. Dr. Karen Tate

"Another world is not only possible, she is on her way. On a quiet day, I can hear her breathing." -Arundhati Roy

When I read that quote for the first time, the breath caught in my throat and the hair stood up on the back of my neck as I remembered...

I had been invited to Wisconsin to present at a weekend workshop which turned out to be a more than wonderful experience. I went thinking I was just going up there to teach these women the workshop material, but the sharing and activities I participated in were a beautifully reciprocal dance. Besides the bonding and the fun, issues I had never quite been able to banish from my psyche had dispersed in the safety of the ritual the night before and I was feeling light and open and gloriously happy and fulfilled.

As the weekend came to a close and the time to drive back to the airport was drawing near, I grabbed a few moments of solitary time behind the dormitory where we were staying located about 100 yards off a serene and shining lake. Between the lake and the dorm, trees had been planted in a circle, with barely two to three feet of space between their trunks, and inside the circle was a bench. I was drawn within the circle desiring a few moments of quiet contemplation in what felt like Nature's embrace.

As I sat there, enjoying a cool breeze on my cheeks, glimpsing the reflection of the sun on the lake between the tree trunks before me, I suddenly realized I heard a rhythmic breathing. In and out. In and out. Where was it coming from? In my mind, I began a process of elimination. I held my own breath for a few moments thinking perhaps here in this small space among this odd configuration of trees I was hearing the echo of my own breath, but no, it wasn't me. I looked around to make sure there was no one else there, perhaps just beyond my initial line of light. No. I wasn't hearing the incoming tide of the lake. I sat there mesmerized as I listened. No, this sound was coming from this very spot where I sat. Dare I ever utter the next thoughts that crossed my mind? It was as if I were sitting within the body of Goddess and I was hearing Her breathing. This was incredulous, but I was going to go with it and just listen, feel, and receive. I soaked in the magic of this sacred place. The hair stood up on the back of my neck and arms. I felt that familiar cold chill up my spine and my tears turned into sobs of joy. What an emotional experience!

In hindsight, many of us might speak in metaphor, as perhaps the novelist and activist Arundhati Roy is speaking above, about Gaia or the coming new paradigm of the Sacred Feminine, but this was different. This experience went beyond metaphor or even feeling inspired in some natural landscape. This wasn't merely equating the ebb and flow of the ocean tides with Her breath as we attempt to personify Her and embrace Her mysteries. This felt as if it were another phenomena of a dimension I had yet to experience. Was I crazy to even contemplate hearing the inhaling and exhaling... of our Mother? Well, sometimes we just have to shut off that left-brain and just feel Her incredible gifts! Those few minutes sitting in that sacred grove in Wisconsin will no doubt be some of the most profound and magickal minutes of my life. Thank you, Mother. Thank you for that precious gift. I can hear you breathing!

My Return to Isis: A Half Century Journey

Bajra (Ann-Lee Waite)

When I was a little girl my very first idol was the goddess Isis. Really. I know, it's the corniest first sentence I have ever written. Smacks of the essays I wrote in middle school! When I returned to college at 30, I took a goddesses of the world course as an elective. I didn't remember my childhood Isis then. By then I was too conditioned into believing in my weakness, in my state of not enoughness. My flame had been dimmed quite a bit. I was still hoping to find a man who would take the responsibilities of living an adult life from me. I was a Cinderella in complex. I wouldn't remember this girlhood idol until I joined a priestess circle at 55.

My family and I were living in Bermuda. It was my first time experiencing having a television in the home. I was seven years old. Before my mother remarried we lived with my grandmother in the Cayman Islands. My mother was a single mother and sometimes I ate ketchup sandwiches because there wasn't anything else to put on the bread. It didn't hurt that I really like ketchup.

I was fascinated with her immediately. I saw myself in her. Her portrayed skin color wasn't far from my own which meant, in my mind, I could be her and she could be me. Years later I would see Isis in the portrayals of Cleopatra and Wonder Woman. I would see the goddess Isis in Harriet Tubman, Maya Angelou, Oprah Winfrey, Frida Kahlo, Joan of Arc, ordinary women with amazing empowerment stories; women who had fought for their right to not just exist but gain their sovereignty to live from their own full expression and not the script handed to her.

Like many women, I struggled with the shaming of my sexual expression; even when you are intelligent and wise enough to question and take apart the shame, early training and conditioning lingers in your mindset. I carried the brand, the scarlet letter of incest and rape because my child mind froze into the belief it was my fault; it had happened because something in me must be WRONG.

By late teens I had created the idea that if I slept with more than five men voluntarily over the course of my LIFETIME that meant I was a slut. I would later move it to 10; after that I knew I was going to hell for sure. I had also learned as a young woman you had to be cautious of who you shared your sexual stories with and you certainly couldn't necessarily trust another woman with it because she received the same training and could, in fact, be an enforcer of slut shaming on behalf of toxic patriarchy.

We expect it from men but not from another woman, so the shaming is often more bitter. We expect the other woman to understand we are attempting, in our own way, to find our sovereignty. I often like to give women more credit for intelligence to see beyond the programming but it's not about intelligence. I was intelligently and systematically programmed. The trauma of rape is a powerful programming tool if you believe another isn't or shouldn't be as powerful as you.

I tested many shame barriers: abortion, multiple sexual partners simultaneously, married men, pushing past the 10 digit total number of sexual partners in a lifetime, a short stint as a stripper, sex on the first date, sex on the first date in the bathroom at a 4 person dinner party and two of them were in the bathroom having sex, sex in exchange for money/shoes/date/new dress/attention/protection/appeasement/shut the fuck up. I was an exhibitionist in how I dressed; I was taught early my value was my body and the sex I could offer. I had been sexually objectified from the time I was five years old. Sex was my currency and my only value. Today I am a fucking miracle. I was a miracle back then too, carrying the seeds of my maternal line: sexual trauma, abuse, dependency, unworthiness.

The things that brought me to Truth were the very same things that had the potential to destroy me. I used to believe marriage and the house with the picket fence were going to save me, were going to wipe me clean. That's what marriage implies in religion: purity. God has touched you sinful woman with purity; in exchange you won't have sex with anyone else or you go back to slutdom. This is your only way out. Or not, as it turns out. Today I'm not clean or dirty. I'm a human woman who survived a world made for her continued servitude to the toxic masculine either through her body or her labor, preferably both.

I used to think sex in my fifties would once again be frequent like in my twenties since I would be free of the chains of social pressure and stigma. While I am free, my evolution has been to discover the true power of sexual intimacy. Did you know you can have a spontaneous awakening during sex? The explosion of love in the heart with orgasm has the possibility of initiating a kundalini awakening!!! The ecstasy of orgasm should have provided the hint of Divine Truth, but we humans are thick. Even intelligence is no match for a thick brain.

When you quash a woman's sexuality, you quash her spiritual connection to God. You squash her ability to awaken to the sovereignty she always had that was there in Isis all the time. A powerful strategy.

Ever since I was a little girl, and I fully believe my early exposure to Isis was responsible, I have had it in my heart to be a free woman and somewhere in my subconscious I knew having sovereignty in my human expression was freedom. I have chosen to remain single, had a child without being married, reclaimed my sexual energy through much trial and error, and with it, my sovereign being. My journey. My way.

As part of my daily spiritual practice I call in the directions and the elements. I ask to be blessed with the qualities I am ready to receive that day and for assistance in releasing what I am ready to release that day. And before starting my morning chant, I read the priestess declaration I created for myself in 2018 as a daily remembering of my true identity as a multidimensional being having a human experience.

Priestess Declaration

As a priestess, I am awoke to the sacredness of every moment. I live in this physical realm fully connected to my true identity as a spirit being.

As a priestess, I acknowledge everything as sacred; seeing beyond the appearance of man's reality.

As a priestess, I lean into the ebb and flow of life-giving energies; I give and receive the blessings of prosperity and wealth of mind spirit and health.

As a priestess, I walk in power and love.

As a priestess, I live between the worlds of man and Spirit. I am both of earth and heaven.

As a priestess, I am all of the elements and from all directions.

As a priestess, I walk the earth as a servant of Spirit.

My qualities are groundedness, wisdom, clarity, creativity, knowledge, inspiration, humor, joy and passion.

My Name is Isis.

Isis: High Priestess

Katherine Skaggs

Mother Goddess Isis, a Love Story

Katherine Skaggs

I had just finished a day with my dear teachers Steven and Jess, at an advanced, energy healing workshop called Circles of Life, sometime in the early 90s. This experiential workshop certainly cleaned my aura and centered me in my heart, leaving me feeling very illuminated and joyful. I went to my hotel room to rest while my dear friend Sharon, who had come to Boulder with me for the workshop, went to dinner with her husband. A short while after she ventured out, I was transported to the Temple of Isis in ancient Egypt in an instant. I was all of a sudden just there! I was dressed in all white, a priestess in the Temples of Isis, at home in the sacred energies of her presence. I also saw Jess and Sharon with me in a place that was certainly home.

Then, just as suddenly, I was back in the hotel room, as Katherine. Astonished, I could not wait for Sharon to come back so I could tell her what happened. It was not a past life memory, it was truly a transportation through time and space to a loving and familiar home in my soul with my Mother Goddess Isis. That night I excitedly shared with my friend, knowing that I also could not wait to tell Jess and Stephen what had happened.

I went to class early the next morning so I could grab Jess and Stephen to tell them of my experience. I found Jess first and got her attention, telling her of this amazing, mystical experience. She looked upon me calmly and knowingly. After my story, Jess said, “Well, yes. And Stephen was there too, also a priestess at that time.” My mouth popped open, as did my eyes go wide. “You saw this too? You were there too????” Calmly Jess said, “Yes.”

That was my first conscious interface with Isis, the sacred Temples of Isis in Egypt, and my deep soul connection. It was not a subtle one. It was not a past life. It was one of the most mystical experiences I could have never in my human mind imagine, where she assisted me in returning home to myself, and to Her.

Over the years I began to pray to Isis, to collect items and sacred objects to represent her in my life. Yet, it wasn't until 2007 that I painted her, when I began my adventure of painting the 22 Goddesses for the Major Arcana in the Mythical Goddess Tarot. The energy of the Divine Mother had come to me over and over since 2003 in mystical experiences to return me to the love and energy of the Divine Feminine.

A second deeply mystical experience came when Mother Mary came to me in 2003 over and over in my inner awareness. I knew I was supposed to paint her, creating a portal of love for all to partake, to activate the heart, to activate the deep, loving presence of the Divine Mother within each of us and this world. This transmission came on the night of the third day where she persisted in getting my attention to paint her. When I went to bed that night, my sleep did not last long, for soon Mother Mary awoke me. I had to get up and paint her then! And then I did so, painting through the night, until almost complete with a 36"x48" acrylic painting.

The magic did not stop there, and I tell you this story of Mother Mary as she is very connected to my deep connection with Great Mother Isis. Multiple times over the next months she came to me again to bring other guidance that was to be written and imprinted into my conscious awareness. During that time I became aware that Mother Mary was a High Priestess in the Temples of Isis and that I indeed knew her too, for she was also born of the love of Isis.

A weaving was taking place, to awaken me in this body, with the vast and deep love of the Great Mother, in various loving ways. This certainly got my attention and began to open my heart, my mind and my own physical being to greater harmony and healing.

Great Mother Isis was indeed working through Mother Mary to bring me love and guidance.

More magic of the Divine Mother unfolded as I was guided to go to Rome in 2006 with two mystical, scholarly, 70-year-old female artists, Lydia Ruyle and Meinrad Craighead. The trip was called "Conversations with the Goddess", Lydia's heart-child "company" that she had formed many trips earlier, devoted to experiential education on the Divine Mother through sacred journeys. From Ephesus in Turkey, to Florence and Rome in Italy, to Paris, France, you could be assured a trip with Lydia Ruyle would bless you with an ancient, timeless understanding of the Divine Mother beyond what the history books have recorded. Upon completion of our trip to Rome, Lydia's words inspired and guided me for the next step in the journey with Isis and all my Divine Mothers, "We have heard History (His Story), now it is time to tell Her-story. Just do it!"

With that I returned home to call my dear friend Sage Holloway, to tell her it was indeed time to create the goddess tarot deck... I finally got the message! For 15 years Sage had told me that she had a Divine Feminine Tarot deck that was to be created and that I was the artist. I would always say, "Yes", only to have time dribble away with no focus on the action of creating it. Now was different, the Great Mother had said, "Just do it!"

With that I painted Goddess after Goddess, with Isis being my focus in 2007. Every time I saw a Goddess, or lower arcana card to paint, I realized I was opening a portal to engage the very energy of that Goddess or card, so it would be available to anyone who gazed upon the art. Every Goddess spoke to me, guided me, and blessed me in my life. Isis, of course was no different. She focused me into her wings and her energies, keeping me captive with her painting for weeks. There were times when I would repaint and redraw entire sections of the painting, as it "wasn't quite right." As I worked the painting visually, so did I work the painting energetically... or rather, it worked me! In 18 months I painted 78 tarot cards, plus design and publication. And of course, Mother Isis was to be on the front cover of the Mythical Goddess Tarot, as the representation of all of the Goddesses and message of the Divine Feminine.

During this time of creating the tarot deck, I stepped deeply upon the path of shamanism in 2007. First, it was of course, to heal myself, and the wounds of relationship, where I held patterns of loss, betrayal and inability to be in a truly loving relationship. Every step along the way I was guided, and Isis was there. I was called to find a famous teacher and author of many books on shamanism. It took a good while as she was on sabbatical writing, but I finally found her teaching at a summer retreat in New Mexico with two other shamanic teachers and two Shipibo shamans from the jungles of Peru. I invested immediately in a spot for myself in a four-day shamanic retreat focused on receiving healing. During that time I did soul retrieval work with this teacher, and found out her guide was Isis! Of course. I didn't think much about it at the time. Yet, looking back I can see the weaving.

I had a fabulous experience, getting a healing from every practitioner, including the two shamans from the jungle. As much as I thought I would continue to do work with Sandra, I was led to do another 10-day training with the other two shamanic teachers. This was again, fabulous and leaving me wanting more as I heard of their advanced, two-year training program. When I asked about registering for the program, or finding out more, I was met with what felt like resistance... "You know this is advanced work." "Well, yeah!" I thought. That is why I am asking! As our conversation proceeded, I found out that part of the program was of course to work with practices and ceremonies that various indigenous peoples worked with, one being plant medicine. Innocently I asked, "How do I sign up?" In August 2007, I sat in my first plant medicine ceremony with the Great Mother plant from the jungles of Peru. In my deep inner journey, I went through a great deal of healing and release of trauma, after which I was ultimately led to Egypt to the Temples of Isis. Once again, I was home.

With such an amazing hair-raising and heart opening experience, I returned again and again over the years to work with this Great Plant Mother, to assist me in healing and awakening. Again and again, I would be with Isis, be told she was my mother, and that I was indeed born of the mystical world of the Temples of Isis. After many years of going to Isis and Egypt over and over, I became profoundly aware of my deep connection to Isis. I knew she and Mother Mary watched over me and guided me. I came to peace knowing they always shine a light on my path and truly, give guidance and protection for the work that comes through my heart, mind and fingers.

One summer, I had an opportunity to sit under the stars in deep inner states in ceremony. At the time I was having dreams and synchronicities with the planet Sirius. I had channeled a painting I call the Sirian, which is the face of what appears as the merging of a humanoid face with a white lion face. I knew it was a guide from Sirius, but didn't know much else about Sirius. So when I entered into ceremony, I asked if I could be shown more about Sirius, and why I was being drawn to this guide and to this "place."

When I began to travel inward, under the vast expanse of the stars, I "shot out" through the stars to Sirius! As I came into this energy, Horus, son of Isis, greeted me. He said, "You are my sister, daughter of Isis." As he welcomed me home, I went into a deep state of peace, bliss and love. I cannot describe the sense of "home" that I had, that I had never felt here on Earth as a human.

As I enjoyed this energy for what is probably several hours of Earth time, I was drawn back to my body to find myself here on Earth, as human Katherine. Oh my goodness, how I wanted to return home to this place I called home, Sirius, home of Goddess Isis.

More than a few years have passed since that summer, with many more visitations of Great Mother Isis. In that time, I have often asked why I can't quite get back to that same experience of home on Sirius, with her and Horus, and the consciousness of many light beings. After I ask, I don't usually "hear" an answer.

However, I do get the answer. The message from the Great Mother Isis to Katherine is:

> "Home is always within, no matter where you are. Home is not across the stars many miles and light years away. Be present.
>
> These experiences are gifts, where you have opened the door to re-membering. Take these experiences and allow them to vibrate through you at all times, transcending yesterday and tomorrow. Do not be distracted by human foibles, angers, fears and differences. Go to the heart of the Great Mother within yourself, that you may give that through your expression, whether it be through your painting, your writing, or your smile and compassionate caring. When you fully embody these energies, you will fully be at 'home' in yourself, and your multidimensionality, with me, with Horus, with all you love.
>
> You are here with me now, AND you are on Earth as this representation and projection of your soul. You are not here or there. You are much bigger than you realize. You have touched on this bigness, on this light, and on the love of who you are, of who I AM. Live your life in the fullness of that love."

I smile, as I sense and know of this transmission of love from the Great Mother Isis. She is with me, as I with her at all times. I am never alone, as you are never alone. She hears my prayers, knows my struggles, as well as my triumphs. She guides me with her gentle yet firm loving light and love. She trusts me that I am growing into fullness and maturity through my experiences, that I am home in the light of love, in the light of wisdom. For as her daughter, she gave me the birthright to have my own adventure of self-discovery, self-empowerment, death and rebirth, and ultimately illumination where I too can shine a light into the world, giving life, giving beauty and giving love.

My experiences and the opening of my heart tell me that this is also your birthright. If you are reading this and find your heart opening through these stories, might I suggest that my stories are also your stories? That within you there is a light awakening, and the call to your own adventures that bring you home to yourself, and to the love of the Great Mother Isis?

Great Mother Isis is the Great Goddess of Death, Birth, Fertility and so much more. She is the Great Mother, benevolent and caring for all her people, her children. I suggest you call upon her and thank her for bringing you to this particular story and any and all ways she is calling to you, letting you know that she is here for you. She is with you and reminding you too, that you are her child, her beloved one, whom she is loving.

If you are courageous enough to do so, ask her to help you die to all the fear, to the old stories of lack, loss and not good enough, so that you may be reborn into love, light and joy once again.

I sincerely send you love of this Great Mother, though I do know, that you are more than capable of feeling it and receiving it within your own very beautiful being.

Isis Banner

Lydia Ruyle

Photo courtesy of the film *Herstory: The Visionary Life of Lydia Ruyle and the Banners of the Divine Feminine* by Isadora Leidenfrost, PhD. A Soulful Media Production. 2019.

In Search of the One Who is Waiting

Donna Snyder

fallen leaves soft as velvet
faded grays and dusky pink
veins dark within decay
humus devoid of warmth
dry leaf upon dry leaf crushed to powder

infant clouds spun of yucca bloom
a basket woven from Earth's bounty
a future full of mystery and chance
the slow kiss of an aging sun
empty vastness of waiting paper

you give birth to the world
the world becomes your lover
a band of gypsies dancing
the beat of hammers mining
percussive shovels dig into earth

possibly saving your own life
late afternoon falls
lost in the experience of tactile pleasure
thought deviates from first thought
returns to earth entwined in vine

you want to cry
you see Isis unveiled

The Path Taken

Susan Morgaine

Whenever we start a journey, we may believe that we know our destination, but in all likelihood, that destination is never firmly discovered until we get there, and even then, there will be detours.

I discovered the Goddess in my mid-teens. I am grateful to my Aunt Norma (my mother's partner) who gave me Sybil Leek's autobiography and set my feet upon the path I have tread since.

Then, for me, the Goddess had no specific name, just Goddess. I had been alone since the death of my Vovo (grandmother) when I was 7 and the Goddess was who I looked to for comfort, as none was coming from my mother.

In my 20's, I began to learn her different names and aspects. I became a student (via books) of Z Budapest, Diane Stein and Starhawk. (Yes, I realize Z has become a lightning rod, but I am still grateful for what I learned from her and was able to tell her this so many years later, when I interviewed her.)

While I began to feel the pull toward Celtic Goddess Spirituality, I felt more immediately drawn to Isis. She called to me; She touched my heart and soul.

Strangely enough, I became closer to Isis while taking an online course called "The Ninth Wave," which at the time was run by Lunaea Weatherstone, founder of *SageWoman* magazine. This was definitely more of a Celtic course, as the Ninth Wave is the way to the Otherworld.

One of the assignments in this course was to stay up all night to find the Goddess that spoke to you, and to find your spiritual name. Again, mine was contradictory. I was called by Isis, but my name was to be Morgaine, as a version of Morgan Le Fey.

I began to work with Isis, and studied all I could about her, while Celtic stayed in the background. I then began to research other Goddesses, Her other aspects around the world. I wanted desperately to connect with a Goddess from Portugal, as my beloved Vovo was from the Azores. While my recent research has been more fruitful, back then, I could find nothing for Portuguese/Iberian/Lusitanian Goddesses.

Through most of my adult life, I worked with many Goddesses, even though I felt I was tied to Isis. I considered myself to be Dianic, as my feminism was strongly tied to my spirituality; they always went hand in hand.

In my search, and research, I discovered Avalon; in this I do not mean any specific Avalonian tradition, but, rather, the idea of the concept of Avalon as a mystical hidden island of women and healing.

I continued to work with Isis and, at the time, felt that She was my matron Goddess. One night before I fell asleep, I looked up toward the ceiling and there She was. She spoke to me and I listened for a long time as I drifted off to sleep. When I awoke, I knew that Isis loved me and called me Her own, and had given Her permission that I follow my heart, wherever it may lead upon this path.

Not long after, I re-discovered that mythical Isle. The pull to Goddesses from the British Isles became stronger. I knew that this was a place I had been before. I felt that I knew Avalon intimately and had been Her priestess many lifetimes ago. My 24 hours awake with "The Ninth Wave" made much more sense to me, as pieces began to fall into place.

There was a brief period filled with personal conflict. I continued working with Isis, continued my search for Portuguese Goddesses, and began to follow my heart to Avalon, which truly was where my heart lay. This was not an easy journey for me, being spiritually pulled in different directions.

With more reading and research, I was ecstatic to find that Portugal, as part of the Iberian peninsula, was considered to be part of the Celtic tribes. For me, two of my three pieces began to merge.

While I do not recommend one tradition over the other, I discovered the Sisterhood of Avalon, waiting ten years to finally join. I have never looked back.

My years of searching have paid off, and I am finally home and at peace with my spirituality and the Goddess/Goddesses I serve, as well as my love for all of my Sisters.

Yet, even with all of the Goddess work and study I had done, until I started to follow my new path, the word "sovereignty" was not even a part of my vocabulary. I knew the word, I knew the meaning of the word, but I had no clue as to how it might pertain to me.

There was no question that I recognized Isis as Sovereign. I was a staunch feminist, but in my day-to-day life, I was a stay-at-home mum, right down to PTO, girl scout leader, cub scout den mother and Unitarian Universalist church board member and leader of their Women's Spirituality Group. While this was the choice I had made for myself, I did not see myself as sovereign in any way.

Being our authentic selves, being our sovereign selves, is one of the things we work toward in the particular Avalon mystery tradition I am in. Using the tools taught to us by our Morgan, we do deep inner work and healing on the path toward our own individual sovereignty.

What does where I am currently in my life and on my spiritual path have to do with our beloved Isis? Looking back at all I have done, studied, and researched, I can see that Isis paved the way to my own sovereignty and, in giving me her blessing to go where my spirit was being led, with her gentle push to follow the path my heart had already chosen was Her way of letting me know this.

I will always worship and honor Isis. She taught me much about myself and the world. To this day, I maintain an altar to Her in a place of honor. I will always be grateful and blessed that She was the first one who chose me as Her daughter and Priestess and that she allowed me to follow my heart and spirit, and the path that I have taken.

The Love of Isis Restores

Hazel DaHealer

Isis represents restorative love. Her love was lost to death yet restored to life. The journey Isis took to restore life to her much-loved Osiris was not a beautiful journey along scenic paths. If we look at the symbolism of her hair being cut and her robes being torn to shreds as she searches for the fourteen pieces of the body of Osiris, we see she is going forth not as a Queen but as someone who is worn down and not at her best.

It's through the process of restoring life that Isis resumes her name as Au Set which roughly translates into 'exceeding Queen.' Her legend presents her wings as protective. Isis is most often depicted with the Ankh which is the ancient symbol of life. She is the bringer of life that was once thought to be lost.

Life during the COVID19 pandemic offers us a chance to revisit Isis and let her story restore our path through the chaos to a place of sovereignty. A lesson we can adapt to our journey is that first we must grieve. We grieve the lives lost to the disease and the lifestyles we lost during this part of our journey. Many of us are privileged to find our main complaints at this time to be the inability to physically gather with our loved ones and the inability to travel unrestricted. We suffer the sadness and stress that comes from not being able to maintain our hair to our usual standards.

Once we realize we are in mourning we can begin our search for wholeness. We can miss the physical contact, but we have the ability to gather via electronic means such as Zoom. We also begin to realize that the external definition of beauty we took on is no longer valid. We see the beauty of the grey blossoming from our untreated hair. We are no longer busy so now our focus shifts to those in our household and those who are our loves.

When we take a look at ourselves and realize we have the ability to reassemble our lives around those we love – and the lifestyle we desire born of our new focus – it is then that we are wrapped in the protective wings of Isis. The new life we bring from the disruption and mourning is like Horus who was conceived through the reassembled parts of Osiris.

Our challenge today is to search out the missing pieces of our lives and reassemble them in a way that restores our lives. Through this restoration, our love of people, places, events, and objects takes on new facets. It's this new life born from loss that makes us stronger. We grow because we somehow sought out what we have lost and recrafted a better way. May Isis restore the love and a more sustainable life to you, your loved ones, and the world that we share! Walk in strength and beauty as the Lady of Ten Thousand names.

Blessed BE!

Isis and Anubis

Tracy Andryc

Ancient Temples: The Heart of Egypt

Rev. Dr. Karen Tate

While it might not be universally accepted, some believe in the concept that we retain memories of other lifetimes within the cells of our DNA. To one who has yet to accept or connect with their old soul or cellular memories of ancient lifetimes, it might seem odd to hear a baby boomer who has lived most of her adult life in Los Angeles say she felt as familiar with the sights, sounds and smells of Egypt as with her West Coast lifestyle, but from my first trip down the Nile, I have had a resonance with this land. Like Om Sety, a modern Osirian priestess from contemporary Britain, the lure of Egypt has always held a fascination, as far back as my pre-school years, perhaps when the veil between memories of past lives is thinnest.

As I sat on the deck of our cruise ship, the Nile Goddess, with golden statues of Isis and Osiris as centerpieces in the lobby, it felt ordained that I should be making this trip with my beloved husband and partner Roy, himself an Anubis-like guardian and walker between the worlds, and with some of my very best friends and sister priestesses. Having spent the last five years as an ordained priestess bringing rituals of the Egyptian Goddess Isis to the community and studying Egyptian mysteries, I felt prepared for this spiritual journey to this ancient land of Kemet. This trip, I was here not to marvel at the ancient stone monuments with the eyes of a tourist, but to feel and experience with the sensibilities of a seasoned priestess, to learn what they had to tell me.

Healing Niches of the Sakkara Temple Complex

After some of our sister travelers availed themselves of the camel rides, some even partaking of some camel kisses from these noble beasts of burden, it was off to the Sakkara temple complex near the Step Pyramid of Zoser, located just outside Cairo, to visit the interesting phenomenon of the healing niches. One person could stand on the last remaining receptor pad while their counterpart would put their head in the stone healing niches of the temples once used by priests for divine guidance in healing and diagnosing illnesses. As would be the case throughout our two week journey, each of us had a somewhat different experience of things mystical. My own experience with the niche could best be described as feeling this emanating energetic sense of chaos and hearing a sound reminiscent of a great motor humming. This powerful sound brought to mind the tremendous energy within the Earth. This was hardly a stretch of the imagination when we were only a few miles away from the pyramids, one of the Seven Wonders of the Ancient World, thought to possess special metaphysical powers; powers this skeptical priestess admits are open to debate but nonetheless continue to be thought-provoking.

The Great Pyramid

Gaining entrance to the inside of the Great Pyramid was a testament to our determination and ingenuity as the Egyptian government had for a time closed the pyramid to private groups, so we counted our blessings and felt lucky indeed to be within this ancient temple! Once inside, we walked up the stairs leading from the pyramid entrance to the Queen's Chamber. Some of us, including myself, focused on chanting an Isis mantra as we ascended, instead of the many steps ahead of us. Once inside the Queen's Chamber, my senses seemed amplified and the space seemed to exude a feminine essence within. As I looked at an immense rock opening leading down another shaft closed to the public, for an instant in my mind's eye, I was stunned to glimpse what I recognized as a giant golden Isis, with feathered wings at her sides, standing there, as if she were a sentinel watching over our visit. I immediately felt what I recognized to be her presence. As if that were not enough to blow one's mind, because I am hardly prone to have these kinds of esoteric experiences very often, I also got a flash of a past life memory. It was me, thousands of years ago, not a woman, but a man, bearing stone burdens to help build the pyramids. I honestly could hear the massive blocks being pulled by ropes and slid into place through these shafts. Prior to these remarkable, and hardly believable experiences, I had rarely had so many intense metaphysical experiences in one place in so short a span of time. Perhaps being in the pyramids did amp up one's psychic abilities! But rather than be a naysayer and skeptic, shutting off the ideas, sights and sounds, I allowed myself to be what Xia, a sister priestess describes as a hollow bone, taking in whatever would come. After all, I could re-examine the experiences at a later time and accept or dismiss the experiences, but if being here was opening awareness, I did not want to foolishly pull the plug.

And this phenomena seemed to be affecting the other women too. I had been told before we departed to trust in the sacred sites and our intuitive abilities to flow with the energy within the temples and pyramids. Perhaps that explained what was happening to us all. With no advance planning, as if by the guidance of an invisible conductor, the women of our group gathered and began singing songs and chants, calling to our Mother Isis. What were the odds we would all know and start singing the same song? It is really hard to describe how being there, feeling what we were feeling, seeing, hearing, and doing affected us. It has been said often that one cannot always use language to describe the Mother; one feels her, senses her and intuits her. I can only say that our group did not enter the pyramid with any expectations. In fact, I did not expect any kind of metaphysical experience here at all, particularly nothing associated with Goddess. My concerns were: Would I be claustrophobic or have trouble climbing the many steps in the airless and hot chamber of the pyramid? Yet it happened to our little group, including me, the resident skeptic. I am not one who is quick to accept such experiences as anything but imagination and wishful thinking unless it comes from a reliable source. Yet, this was all real. The intensity of the experience moved us to tears of joy in the ecstasy of the moment, but we did not have time to linger. The guide was coming and we had to quickly set aside these sensations to begin to ascend the steps to the Kings Chamber.

Once there, we took turns lying in the sarcophagus and discussing the possible use of the pyramids as a place for initiations of the ancient priesthood learning the great mysteries of Osiris. These mysteries would show the initiate the separation between the flesh and blood vessels of our body and our soul or psychic self that continues on beyond the death. One could only speculate on having the privilege to experience the revelations and rebirth from having spent many hours in trance here within the pyramids where these secrets might be revealed. And perhaps while we were in the Queen's Chamber we had been gifted with a glimpse into these mysteries.

Philae – Island of the Temple of Isis

Having left the wonders of Cairo, with its museums, bazaars and traffic, we were off to Aswan for a visit to beautiful Philae Island, home of the Isis Temple, which stood on the outskirts of the territory between Egypt and Nubia. Isis is here in her warrior aspect, blended with Sekhmet, the lion-headed warrioress and healing Goddess so important to women today. Both protect the borders of Kemet, their great land.

We arrived by felucca, a traditional sailing boat used along the Nile. We were dressed in our priestess garb of white linen with our sistra, or sacred rattles, readily at hand and prepared for ritual. We entered the inner chamber, the cella, or holy of holies, of Isis' temple at Philae, on a glorious morning. At her altar, the heart of the Goddess, surrounded by beautiful hieroglyphic scenes which somehow escaped the fanatic destruction that was the fate of the images on the exterior of the temple, we began the first part of our ritual. Tears welled in my eyes and the hair stood on the back of my neck as the energy surged amongst us as we recited the ancient Egyptian words of power in this inner sanctum. As was typical, our time alone in these holy places was all too short so we progressed to an area nearby that once supported a Coptic church. Here we continued our reverence and revelry witnessed by many who observed in quiet awe.

Around our makeshift altar we danced, chanted and anointed ourselves. Amidst the sweet tinkling of our sistra, we called on Isis in her most ancient names to grant us that which we seek. We cast our petitions and prayers into the flames of the cauldron, later casting the ashes, along with our offerings of bread and beer, into the life giving waters of the Nile.

The prevailing senses collectively experienced by our entourage was that of familiarity and a feeling of belonging, which made leaving bitter sweet. We felt we had certainly been a part of this temple long ago, probably doing some of these very same things in our roles as devotee or clergy of Isis, even though this beautiful temple no longer stood on its original foundation. The energy and ancient memories must have permeated the very stones. As our boat pulled away from the island, our eyes lingered on our ancient home, our souls remembering being together in the past as we were here this very special day.

Sekhmet Temple of Karnak

With all that had transpired in this short week, one could hardly expect more, yet our most powerful connections were made within the Sekhmet Chapel of Karnak, near Luxor. The temple of this lion-headed Goddess of healing and war was in an area off-the-beaten-path of most tourists, where entrance must be gained through negotiation with the guards at the site. There encircling her seven foot tall intact statue, lighted only by a small slit in the stone ceiling allowing in natural light, you could feel the ancient walls still vibrated with her power as the ten of us danced, sang, and chanted mantras, all geared toward raising our energy levels and that within the temple to praise and invoke Sekhmet. We made offerings of candles and incense to this Goddess of healing, tenacity and empowerment, asking her to bestow her gifts upon us and our loved ones whose pictures we brought and placed at her feet.

For me, I lit the red candle given to me long ago at my initiation when I pledged to stand in my own power. I invoked Sekhmet, asking her to bestow upon me that which I might need to continue my work as a contemporary priestess of the Goddess. As when I was in the Great Pyramid, I shut off my critical mind, and allowed in the thoughts and sensations directed toward me. In a light trance, it seemed I sensed her energy like a white smoke enter within from my yoni. It seemed to travel through my womb up to my solar plexus as her essence filled me.

But the energy of this place was different for each of us. Roy gleaned it was a "women-only" space and his presence was accepted by the great Goddess because she recognized he was guardian and brother to the women in this entourage.

Moondancer felt the walls go liquid and could barely stand as the euphoria almost overcame her. Sekhmet priestess, Shakti, felt her heart chakra open and she became a vessel to help heal certain women with us for whom she had not previously known needed healing.

The small, darkened chapel seemed to vibrate with the intensity of feeling and knowing that could hardly be described in words. And while these esoteric experiences may raise an eyebrow or two, they are far from isolated incidents. Others who have come to Egypt have sworn to seeing statues of Sekhmet move their head, or otherwise normal people have had auditory experiences they defined as messages from Goddess. Petitions and pledges to Goddess have been heard and answered just as on any more traditional pilgrimage. Should those devoted to the Divine Feminine be denied experiences with their deity similar to those recounted by devotees of God over thousands of years? I think not. It is all just a matter or perspective.

Bubastis and Alexandria

Another rarely visited site, barely as yet unearthed, was Bubastis, meaning House of the Goddess Bastet. This archaeological site was not only home to her ancient temple but also of the feline graveyards of Tel Basta. This was one of the most ancient cities in Egypt, and according to Herodotus it gave one pleasure to look upon it. This high praise seemed to be both for the temple itself and because the city all around it had been raised to a higher level, so you could look down upon the temple where it stood amid shade trees on almost an island formed by two embracing canals which stopped short without meeting. Contemporary political controversy blocks meaningful restoration of the site, yet travelers can visit a small museum and glimpse a sacred well covered merely by a rough-hewn wooden cover. No temples have as yet been reconstructed, yet one can see among the tall grasses the landscape of granite blocks decorated with inscriptions and reliefs awaiting the end of human bureaucracy so that progress might begin.

Off to the side of this field of stones visitors could see the remains of the underground galleries for the burial of cats where ancient bronzes of cats had been found. It was here among the mud brick walls and enclosures we did our worship to Bastet, Soul of Isis, asking her blessing for our beloved feline children.

Leaving Bubastis, traveling north toward the Mediterranean Sea, our destination was Alexandria, known in antiquity for its famous library, a center of knowledge in the ancient world and home to one of the most famous queens of Egypt, Cleopatra VII, also a priestess of Isis. When we visited, the Egyptian government was in the process of building a new library in this ancient-modern city with the hope it will some day house one copy of each book in our known world. Several years and over $220 million later, the Bibliotheca Alexandria is a reality, with its mission to be a center of excellence in the production and dissemination of knowledge and to be a place of dialogue, learning and understanding between cultures and peoples. According to the literature, the unique role of the contemporary library of Alexandria is similar to its predecessor, with added international dimensions. The library is the world's window on Egypt and Egypt's window on the world. It is a leading institution of the digital age and a center, where ISIS, the International School of Information Science, is based. Located in the Eastern Harbor, facing the sea, overlooking the Silsilah Peninsula, it stands near the Pharos Lighthouse, one of the Seven Wonders of the Ancient World, and very close to the site of the ancient library that was believed to be located within the Brucheion, or Ancient Royal Quarter.

Not far from the new library, along the shores of the city of Alexandria, we got as close as possible to the site where the Temple of Isis once stood and Cleopatra sat upon her throne. As we gazed out upon the sea, we knew the stones from that temple complex lay beneath the waters of the harbor just a few hundred yards beyond where we stood, where Cleopatra first set her gaze upon Julius Caesar.

Later, at the Greco-Roman Antiquities Museum of Alexandria, our Isian sisterhood had their fancies tickled with the many rarely seen artifacts of Isis from that period. We also visited the unique catacombs beneath Alexandria which were like a labyrinthine city of the dead underneath the modern city streets. With many tombs in restored condition we could gaze upon splendid murals of Egyptian and Greek death cult scenes, offering us a unique glimpse into the life under the rule of the Ptolomies. Exciting too, was standing on the site of the great Pharos Lighthouse, allowing the spray of the Mediterranean to brush our faces as we imagined fleets of antiquity docking in the harbor bringing travelers to Alexandria from all parts of the civilized world.

Abydos – Temple of Osiris

Before leaving for Egypt, most of us had devoured the book *In Search of Om Sety*, by Jonathan Cott, who revealed the story of a modern woman who spent the better part of her life, until her death in the 1980s, as a priestess of Osiris. She spent many hours each day in and around the Temple of Osiris in Abydos working for the Egyptian Antiquities Department and practicing the old religion of the ancient Egyptian gods and goddesses. With our passions and imaginations ignited, our visit to what is believed to be one of the most ancient of all the Egyptian temples was an experience none of us will forget in our lifetime.

Just getting to Abydos was an adventure as access was restricted and we needed a military escort wearing bulletproof vests the entire way. At the temple itself, as we walked the outer perimeter of the temple and surrounding ruins, we were guarded by soldiers on camels. They added to the surreal nature of our experience with their machine guns ever ready across their laps as they rode upon their noble beasts. They were there to protect us from any terrorist threats, however, never did we feel threatened. In fact, everywhere we went, dressed in our cool white linen galabayas, the locals were respectful and asked if we had come there to pray. If there were some risks involved coming here, we all felt it was worthwhile because promise of the secrets of the Temple of Osiris felt just beyond the veil of our modern sensibilities.

Somewhat of an enigma-defying explanation is the 4,000 year old stone carving which seems to depict a modern tank and helicopter. Other mysteries of the temple were hinted at by Om Sety, and interestingly, without knowing about those specific references in Cott's book, my psychic husband sensed that beneath the temple floor was a chamber yet to be revealed to modern archaeology. At the rear of the temple is the Osirion where we could see but not reach the healing waters used by Om Sety. The mystery that seemed to emanate from these ancient stones of the Osirion seemed to beckon you within, though unfortunately, entrance there is denied to tourists. The sense of magic and wisdom felt almost tangible here in Abydos, with the keys to knowledge laying just beyond reach and awaiting discovery. We could only hope the temple might yet offer up more of its secrets in our lifetime.

As was the case so often on this trip, we only wished we had more time to spend there, to do ritual and perhaps spend the night. We could totally understand Om Sety living out her days in this powerfully magical place that seemed as if it might, any second slip through an early morning mist and disappear into the folds of time.

In Retrospect

This journey was a revelation on many levels from the mundane to the magical. Never will we forget the black crows that followed us from place to place so reminiscent of Horus, the hawk-headed son of our beloved Isis, especially the one that would awaken me in the mornings tapping the glass of our hotel window in Aswan. Carved into my memory forever will be the beautiful Hathor-headed columns of the Temple of Hathor at Dendera and the magnificently restored tomb of Queen Nefertari in the Valley of the Queens. And the utter chaos at the airports at Ramadan, the Muslim holy month, will never leave my memory.

Months and years after the journey, the effect was still with me. Our experiences, though out of the ordinary, and perhaps even a little bizarre by traditional standards, were real. Yet are they much different from visions and epiphanies documented by ancient, even biblical scribes? I know for myself the strength and courage I felt permeate my being in the presence of Sekhmet in her temple at Karnak. That resolve seemed to steel and guide me through trials and transformations that challenged me in the time beyond this journey, helping me find strength to stand in my truth and integrity. As long as my red candle of initiation lasts, it will light other flames in ritual for healing and strength.

Remembering our Egyptian pilgrimage, the cool breeze of the Nile blowing through my hair on the sun deck of the Nile Goddess, sipping cold hibiscus tea, I wondered then as I do now, what other journeys lay ahead as we journeyed together to seek out the Divine Feminine in all her sacred locales.

**Originally published in the award winning, *Walking An Ancient Path; Rebirthing Goddess on Planet Earth*, by Rev. Dr. Karen Tate.

The Ankh - Music of Life Sistrum

Trista's Sistrum, handmade by Mike Turner of Kentaurus Designs Shop.
Photo by Anders Løberg

The Sistrum: Sacred Rattle of Creation

Rev. Dr. Karen Tate

According to the Greek philosopher, Plutarch, the sacred rattle or sistrum, used by the ancient clergy of the Egyptian Goddesses Hathor, Isis and Bast, kept the energy of the universe flowing. Shaking sistra literally kept the four elements of air, fire, water and Earth, in a generative state and kept chaos at bay.

Interestingly, the Goddess Isis, often called Nature, or the first matter, was often referred to as the essence of the four elements. Some Hermetic depictions of her have her wearing a girdle of four golden plates representing life, light, heat and force, which generated all things. By her own statement as recounted by Apuleius in *The Golden Ass*, Isis is queen of all the elements. The Knot of Isis, a knotted fabric of cloth on the upper torso of images of Isis and her clergy, has been said to represent the underlying unity of the four elements. It stands to reason then, that as Goddess Advocates begin to reconstruct Goddess Spirituality, especially if they are interested in the Egyptian pantheon, the sistrum and its use would inspire a reintroduction of the instrument into contemporary spiritual practices.

There are several styles of sistra. They were primarily women's ritual percussion instruments. Some of the earliest may have been a box containing loose objects, including a pod-like flower with seeds inside or bundles of papyrus flowers. Later, the sistra were made of a ceramic-like faience, metal, or even clay. A naos sistrum had a shrine-like top often depicting the head of the Goddess Hathor. These more fragile ceremonial types of sistra might have been thought to be a manifestation of Goddess. In the hands of a priestess, the mortal female became elevated to personify the Earthly embodiment of the Creatrix.

The metal sistra were usually ankh shaped, with a metal loop set atop a handle, intentionally suggestive of the hieroglyphic significance of the ankh as a symbol of life. Further, as the sistrum was believed to have the power of regeneration, it makes sense the loop could be considered a womb and the handle a phallus. Providing additional layers of meaning, in hermetic or alchemical terms, Isis was viewed as the Natural Law suggesting productivity is attained by means of polarity. As wisdom personified, Isis was often depicted standing between the pillars of opposites to demonstrate that understanding is found in equilibrium. Isis has also been known to represent justice because Nature is eternally consistent, thus in some of her imagery she is shown with a pair of scales. Thus this sacred instrument of Isis is the symbol of the feminine principle in harmony with the male principle, and the divine blending and equilibrium of natural forces. Dare this author suggest the Goddess Isis might herself personify the balance and equality of masculine and feminine forces of the universe within herself? On a temple wall in the city of Sais an inscription read, "I, Isis, am all that has been, that is or shall be; no mortal Man hath ever me unveiled."

These metal hooped or arch shaped sistra (from the Greek word to shake) were known in ancient Egypt as sesheshet, a word which is thought to recall, by onomatopoeia, the rustling sound it makes. It has been said this rustling sound was like that of Hathor walking through papyrus plants. Sometimes the sistrum's tones might be compared to a tambourine as the sounds from the instruments might be described to range from a light tinkling to a loud jangling. The sound came from either the metal bars that ran horizontally through the naos or loop being struck, or the discs that were sometimes attached to the bars being shaken. It is thought the beat of the sistrum was three beats followed by a pause. It has been said the musical notes associated with the sistra might have been as follows: Air = Mi and B, Fire = Re and D, Water = T and E and LA, Earth = Do and So

Other features carved or affixed on the sistrum might be spirals that framed the sides of the naos to represent the horns of Hathor in her bovine aspect. Imagery of papyrus, royal cobras, and the Egyptian God Bes might be worked into the motif on handles. Cats were sometimes placed atop the metal loop versions of sistra. Plutarch elaborated on the human face on the cat atop the sistra suggesting it represented the intellectual and reasonable nature of the changes that take place in connection with the moon. So it might be said the ebb and flow of the universe, the waning and waxing of the moon, the Earth changes, the tides, are all encompassed within the musical instrument of the sistrum. Certainly not just a mere musical instrument.

Besides embodying Goddess and its use, keeping the energies of the Earth flowing, the sound was believed to keep evil at bay and was believed to have a satisfying and pacifying affect on mortals and gods alike. An inscription on the walls at the Temple of Denderah reads, "I dispel what is hostile by means of the sistrum in my hand." Priestesses touched the hands of onlookers with their sistra thereby bestowing blessings upon them. The sistrum was an emblem of the priestess' authority given to her at the Ritual Presentation of the Emblems. It was believed in this ceremony that Hathor transmitted the essence of her divinity to the sacred ornament and became that ornament. When the ornament was passed to the priestess during this ritual, the Divine essence of Goddess merged with priestess, and the mortal woman thus earned the right to bear the title Hathor. In the Temple of Amun-Re at Karnak, the sistrum was utilized in ritual by the priestess of Hathor, representative of the procreative element, to sustain the gods virility. It was also shaken to avert the flooding of the Nile. The sistrum was believed to be a gift to the Goddess Bast from her Divine mother Isis. Used like a bell, the sound invoked positive vibrations and dispelled the negative. The sistrum was usually shown being used in the right hand and when properly tuned, the sistrum was thought to be able to call in the vibration of Isis.

Today the sistrum is in use beyond Goddess Spirituality communities. It is still used by Kemetic practitioners and in Coptic and Ethiopian churches. During ritual, clergy in Coptic churches direct the sistrum at the four cardinal points (which are directly associated with the four elements) to demonstrate the extent of God's creation. Musical groups and churches sometimes still use the sistrum when they want to arouse movement and activity and encourage ecstatic energy. In Goddess Spirituality communities, the sistrum can be an invaluable tool with many uses within and without ritual; some being to generate energy, as a ceremonial object, to purify space or simply for the sweet sound it makes, especially if copper discs are used.

The Heraklion Museum on the island of Crete displays the earliest known sistrum from that area; it was made of clay with only two horizontal rods and two disks per rod still apparent. Inspired by that ancient sistrum and a class given by Priestess Brenda Matarazzo, I have continued the tradition by giving various classes on making small clay sistrum for one's personal use, as well as metal sistra similar to the aforementioned ancient ones for more public ritual.

You can make a sistrum of clay with supplies purchased from your local crafts store, but for durability I recommend metal. For detailed information on creating your own metal sistrum, you are referred to deTraci Regula's book, *Mysteries of Isis*, obtainable at your local bookstore. Museum replicas of ancient sistra can be purchased from the Athens Museum in Greece. Call the Greek Consulate in Los Angeles or New York for more information on reaching the Athens Museum.

What follows are directions to make a smaller and personal ceremonial sistrum of clay.

Making Clay Sistra

Materials Needed:

- 1 box of Sculpey Clay from your local crafts store. Choose the color of your liking. I can suggest a terra-cotta color.
- Approximately 24" of 12-gauge solid copper wire.
- 20 disks—these should be very light.
- 8 decorative beads (optional).

Suggestions: Cut disk from a very light and thin sheet of copper. Use flattened bottle caps. I used very light coin-looking accent pieces normally sewn on costumes. Get creative and use your imagination. A hole needs to be drilled into the center of each disk. The costume accessories sometimes already have a hole at the top where it was intended to sew the disk to clothing. You can use this hole even though it is not in the center.

Using the general dimensions of approximately 8-10 inches in length (5-inch handle and 5-inch oval). The center of the oval should be approximately two to four inches wide. The thickness of the frame of the clay all around the rim should be one to two inches. Use this as a guide. You may have to experiment.

Shape the clay to your desired size and thickness, keeping in mind simple shapes work best. The technique that worked best for me was to shape clay by forming one long rope-like length. Next I looped over the oval, joining the two ends at the handle area for securest adhesion. This is a crucial joint so you must take care to insure the clay is blended well.

After you have the desired shape, make the holes the wire will run through, then follow the directions on the box of clay for baking.

To make the holes, take a wire, skewer or ice pick slightly larger in circumference than the 12-gauge wire, and from the outer rim of the oval of the sistrum, run it through the center of the oval in four places on each side of the oval rim through to the other outer rim directly opposite. The end result should be four sets of parallel holes, which enable you to run four pieces of the 12-gauge wire level and horizontally from side to side of the rims of the oval. It is on each of these four pieces of wire that you will put your disks.

Make sure your clay has baked the appropriate time and cooled. Do not rush this process for maximum durability of the clay. Cut your wire into four pieces of equal length, approximately six inches each. Run a piece of wire through each set of horizontal holes, putting five disks on each wire. Finish the ends with a twist or bend the wire on the outer side of the rim. On each piece of wire end you can attach a very light decorative bead or talisman (optional). Keep in mind that the disks should not be too heavy and should be in proportion to the size of the sistrum.

You can paint or decorate your sistrum to make it your own creation. You might even paint the disks copper or gold if you used bottle caps. You might consider painting Egyptian designs on the sistrum or gluing a talisman like a scarab to the sistrum. Do not be afraid to let your creative juices flow!

Note the significance of the number of bars and discs used: The four parallel bars represent the four elements of air, fire, water and Earth. The five disks on each represent the four elements and spirit.

Now you are ready to use your personal sacred rattle of Isis, Bast or Hathor at your own altar or in your own ritual. Use the rattle to punctuate prayer, to invoke positive energy, to dispel negative energy or simply to honor Goddess with the lovely sound of the tinkling disks. To get started, what follows is an invocation of Isis and Anubis, representative of the male and female principles.

Invocation of Isis and Anubis

Hail Isis, Magnificent One
Mother of all the Domain
Goddess of Ten Thousand Names
Blessed are you among the Goddesses.
Today I raise my voice and sing praise to you!
(Shake Sistrum)

Isis, Eses, Auset
Watch over your priestess today and always.
Help her be of service to you and her community.
Allow her to learn and know more of you.
Great Mother, watch over my loved ones who need your care.
(Shake Sistrum)

Anubis, great guide and protector, help show me the way.
Help me to distinguish the wheat from the chaff.
Guide me to flow with life's synchronicities.
So that I may know my destiny.
(Shake Sistrum)

Isis, you who are Wisdom and Nature, may your golden wings embrace me.
Anubis, Golden One, cast your light upon my path.
Together, teach me the divine balance of the universe.
With your blessing, so shall it be.
(Shake Sistrum)

*Article originally appeared in the award-winning, *Walking An Ancient Path; Rebirthing Goddess On Planet Earth* by Karen Tate.

Photograph by Karen Tate,
Louvre Museum in Paris.

Reclaim Her Name[65]

Susan Morgaine

Inscription from Isis' Temple at Sais:

I am Isis, mistress of the whole land... I am she who separated the heaven from the earth. I have instructed mankind in the mysteries. I have pointed out their paths to the stars. I have ordered the course of the sun and the moon. I am queen of the rivers and winds and sea. I have brought together men and women. I gave mankind their laws. I have made justice more powerful than silver and gold. I have caused truth to be considered beautiful. I am she who is called the Goddess of women. I, Isis, am all that has ever been, that is or shall be; no mortal man hath ever me unveiled. The fruit which I have brought forth is the sun.

You will need an altar specific to Isis, a bell, 1 blue candle, 1 white candle, 1 black candle, and a mirror.

Set up your altar and create sacred space in whatever manner you do personally.

Stand (or sit) before your Isis altar and close your eyes. Breathe in deeply through the nose and exhale. Bring all of your visual focus to Isis. Deeply inhale Her presence. Exhale. Deeply inhale the Breath of Isis. Exhale. Ask Isis for Her blessing and open yourself to her, all the while continuing to breathe in Her presence.

---

65 I wrote this ritual a few years ago for use in my Goddess Spirituality workshop on Isis when the Islamic State was at its' height.

****Ring the Bell****

*****Light the blue candle and say****

All Hail Isis—
Maiden, Mother, Crone.
You, who were there in the beginning and from whom all things come.
I call upon you—
Bless this sacred space with your presence.

All Hail Isis—
Goddess of Ten Thousand Names.
You who are all things—
the air we breathe, the water that is our blood—
the sacred earth beneath our feet, the fire that is our spirit.
I call upon you—
Bless this sacred space with your presence.

All Hail Isis—
Giver of Life and Rebirth,
You whose magic made the world.
I call upon you—
Bless this sacred space with your presence.

****Stop here and once again do the beginning breath sequence*****

All Hail Isis—
I come before you today
to beseech you to reclaim your name.
Reclaim and be made stronger once again—
As this candle burns.

As the flame flickers and becomes strong and steady,
so, too will your presence once again become a beacon
in the world.
Isis, weave your magic.
So Shall It Be.

****Light the White Candle****

All Hail Isis—
Reclaim your name,which has been stolen from you
to be used for the evil that men do.
As this candle burns—
As the flame flickers, the evil that has co-opted our name will
diminish and disappear as the candle disappears.
Isis, weave your magic.
So Shall It Be.

****Light the Black Candle****

Sit quietly before the altar, bringing your attention to the candles and to your own intentions. Do this for as long as it is comfortable for you. When done, inhale deeply and say:

All Hail Isis—
Goddess of Ten Thousand Names.
You who were there in the beginning
and from whom all things come.
I give thanks and honor for your presence within this sacred space.
Be in Peace, Be in Peace.

****Ring the bell****

MEDITATION TO FOLLOW RITUAL

Bring yourself to a lying down position and make sure you are comfortable. Put a bolster beneath your knees to protect your back, if necessary.

Close your eyes and begin to breathe long and deep through your nose.

As you inhale, visualize your deepest self opening up; as you exhale, let go of all stress and tension. Inhale and open yourself to wisdom and beauty; exhale and let go of all negative emotions and images of yourself.

Slowly move your focus to deep within you, to your heart center, the center of your very being. Continue to breathe long and deep. With each breath, allow yourself to go deeper and deeper into your heart.

Open yourself to the Goddess, to Isis, the Divine One. Allow her and welcome Her into your heart, your spirit, your very being.

Keeping your eyes closed, you feel a bright light. Your deep self hesitates to open your eyes for fear that it will burn, but slowly you do and find yourself bathed in a warm, silvery glow. You are peaceful, calm and you feel Her presence enveloping you.

You rise as She walks toward you, opening Her arms to welcome you. What do you need from Her? What wisdom are you looking for? Take time to ask Her and listen to what She may tell you. Breathe deeply now; She is with you. Stay with Her as long as you wish.

As the light starts to fade, you bow your head and thank Her.

Breathing slowly and deeply through your nose, you start to gently bring the awareness back into your body. Move your body gently, open your eyes and know She is with you always.

Look deeply within your mirror. Look at your reflection – you are a daughter of the Goddess. You are the daughter of Isis.

"There, in the beginning was Isis, Oldest of the Old, She was the Goddess from whom all becoming arose. She was the Great Lady, Mistress of the Two Lands, Mistress of Shelter, Mistress of Heaven, Mistress of the House of Life. She was the Unique. In all Her great and wonderful works, She was a wiser magician and more excellent than any other."

- R. E. Witt

Isis's Initiation: Taking Your Throne[66]

Syma Kharal

Pre-Initiation Preparation:
Advance prep: if you can, buy yourself a crown, tiara, or garland, as well as a rattle (or simply make your own rattle by adding rice in a sealed container).

Adorn your altar with flowers, incense, crystals, candles, or anything you feel guided to.

Wear a fancy dress, one that makes you feel like a queen.

Adorn yourself with beautiful makeup, jewelry, the crown if you have it, and perfume.

Use your nicest chair or cover a regular chair with a beautiful cloth.

Play ancient Egyptian music in the background.

Isis's Initiation: Taking Your Throne

Ritual Type: Guided Meditation

Sit on your adorned chair in all your regal attire. Close your eyes and chant the ancient Kemetic invocation to Isis, "*Dua Isis*" or "*Dua Ast*" three times (*dua* means "I invoke/praise/give thanks

66 This chapter is from Syma Kharal's book, *Goddess Reclaimed: 13 Initiations to Unleash Your Sacred Feminine Power,* which thoroughly discusses 13 Goddesses and culminates with an extensive chapter on Isis. This particular initiation is a celebration and integration of all the previous Goddesses they have "activated" along the journey. The editors recommend purchasing the book and working through it in its entirety.

to") as you shake your rattle. Rest your hands on your lap now, still holding the rattle if you wish.

Listen to the music you have chosen for this initiation. Let it move through you, transporting you instantly into the inner realms. See yourself arriving at the doors of a royal temple palace. It is lined with tall, majestic columns inscribed with the wisdom of all the Goddesses.

Announce yourself as:
"I Am (your name), daughter of (your mother's name), granddaughter of (both your grandmothers' names)."

The door opens and you are welcomed in by regal priestesses. At the throne, you see glorious Isis waiting for you with Her arms and wings outstretched.

She draws you to Her, and now you are right with Her. She wraps you in Her protective wings, and you feel the embrace of the Great Goddess enfold you. Melt into Her as the Queen Mother Goddess holds you with deepest reverence and love.

She says She has been waiting a long time to welcome you back, to appoint you on your rightful seat upon your throne, where you have always belonged.

She calls in all the Divine Feminine aspects of Herself, all aspects of yourself, and they appear as infinite Goddesses—the thirteen other Goddesses you have already met and countless more.

They begin to offer you, Their fellow sister Queen Goddess, Their unique gifts of love.

They bestow upon you the sacred spiral, the endless abyss through which all comes through.

They gift you with the flower of life, which bears the seeds for all of creation.

They gift to you the Divine spark, so that you may transform and transmute what doesn't serve you.

They gift to you the chalice of holy water, so that you may heal and bless all you need to.

They gift to you the sword of truth, so that you may overcome all inner and outer obstacles with fierce grace.

They gift to you a shower of gold, so that abundance may flow forth from your Divine center.

They gift to you the quill of creation, so that you may express your highest inspirations.

They gift to you the lotus flower, so that you may rise above all heartaches and trials.

They gift to you a magical wand, so that you may will your desires into miraculous manifestations.

They gift to you the holy fruit—the red apple—so that you may awaken to the feminine mysteries.

They gift to you the sacred serpent, so that you may unleash your full *shakti* force.

They gift to you the wise owl, so that you may resurrect your spiritual powers.

They gift you with bountiful more blessings. Receive them graciously as you sit in your Queenly worth and value.

In groups, the Goddesses come before you. They are here to bless you. They are here to *be you.*

Isis now invites all Goddesses of the void and sacred silence to merge with you.

Isis invites the Goddesses of the underworld and heaven to merge with you.

Isis invites the Goddesses of feminine wrath and transformation to merge with you.

Isis invites the warrior Goddesses of liberation and empowerment to merge with you.

Isis invites the Goddesses of grace and compassion to merge with you.

Isis invites the Goddesses of Divine love, pleasure, passion, sexuality, and joy to merge with you.

Isis invites the Goddesses of aspiration, inspiration, and self-realization to merge with you.

Isis invites the Goddesses of wisdom, strategy, and action to merge with you.

Isis invites the Goddesses of freedom, integrity, and honor to merge with you.

Isis invites the Maiden-Mother-Crone Triple Goddesses of womb wisdom to merge with you.

Isis invites the Goddesses of abundance, sustenance, and support to merge with you.

Isis invites the Goddesses of healing, miracles, magic, and creativity to merge with you.

Isis invites the Goddesses of the sun, moon, stars, earth, and all of creation to merge with you.

She initiates you once and for all as the Divine Creatress, Priestess, Warrioress, Maiden, Mother, Crone, Lover, Muse, Life-giver, Destroyer, Transformer, Transmuter, Initiator, Leader, Wild Woman, Huntress, Oracle, Seer, Sorceress, Magician, Alchemist, Miracle Worker, Witch, Midwife, Healer, Sustainer, Nourisher, Enchantress, Savioress, Protectress, and Empress.

She places Her crown upon your head and initiates you as the Sovereign Queen Goddess of all that you are. She appoints royal councils and priestesses to serve and support you as you commit to serving and leading on your Divine path.

Seated regally on your throne, you now radiate out all your Sacred Feminine powers from the Goddesses that have merged within you, the Goddesses that you are. Behold as your entire Queendom and all those in it are blessed and uplifted as you are. See now your Goddess essence radiate out in blessing to all.

As you bless all beings everywhere, Isis spreads Her wings again, and showers you with blessings, which pour forth as shimmering *ankhs* (Her sacred symbol of life, drawn as the circle-headed cross).

Isis shares with you a loving message to empower you to transmit this initiation as Queen into your earthly life. Receive Her guidance.

Isis now merges Her holy self with you. Her wings become your wings. Her powers become your powers. She is you. You are Her. She is the Goddess. You are the Goddess.

Come back now, beloved. Slowly, gently. Heart open and head held high. To live as Queen in all of your lives.

Post-Initiation Self-Care:

Seal in this ritual by shaking Her rattle as you dance in sacred celebration.

Continue to spend your day in your regal attire.

Ground this final initiation with Goddess rituals: walking barefoot on the earth, bathing in sea salt water, eating a decadent meal—whatever you feel guided to.

Write down the next inspired steps you will take to assume your leadership and sovereign power.

Celebrate the completion of your journey through intuitively guided ceremony: prayer, meditation, a day at the spa or in nature, or a champagne toast to yourself!

Continue to honor your Goddess nature every day, for all the Goddesses live through you now.

Affirming Isis:
I am the Sacred Mistress.
I am the High Priestess.
I am the Heavenly Creatress.
I am the Dark Destructress.
I am the Fearless Warrioress.
I am the Swift Savioress.
I am the Holy Loveress.
I am the Magical Sorceress.
I am the Fierce Protectress.
I am the Wild Huntress.
I am the Intoxicating Enchantress.
I am the Sovereign Queen and Empress.

I am the One and All Goddess.

I Am Isis.

The Sight of Isis

Nuit Moore

I harvest breath, gallows' gold,
phosphorescence dusky glow,
a potion of transformation.

The eyes of Isis,
the Veil of the Black Isis
is lifted by this initiation.
Her eyes button the forest floor
and hold the keys to nevermore.

I take her eyes into my mouth.
Light as a moth and salted earth
dissolves as the veil ascends
and
the sacred dance of Isis begins.
Pure.
Multifaceted ultraviolet depths to delight,
the velvet folding veils of the night
beaming through my eyes.

The dance is made of mystery,
cyclic reverb of dark and light,
the mystic flight of Isis over many lands.

Her eyes glow and seethe with pleasure-
Her eyes indeed do measure
the weight of the soul.
The secret to that skill
shall never be told.

My eyes breathe with the sight of Isis.
Her eyes dissolve through me,
my blood is regal psychedelic gold.
I silently glide through the mossy veils,
as I spot her silver moon boat here,
there – through sliver of sky sight.
Nymph footed fleeting slide
through the shady vale.
Her great luminous lunar eye
at my back, my mouth, my sides.
Her breathing parts my veil
and prophecies twine
about the buzzing threads of my hair.

Towards dawn her breath will depart,
moving from this place to another.

Another night I will consume again
the psychic eyes of my mother.

Anubis, Isis, Osiris

Tracy Andryc

Separate, Then Together: The Alchemical Roots of Sacred Partnership in Egyptian Mythology[67]

April C. Heaslip, PhD

This too is an experience of the soul
This dismembered world that was the whole god
Whose broken fragments now lie dead.
This passing of reality itself is real.

Beyond the looming dangerous end of night
Beneath the vaults of fear do his bones lie,
And does the maze of nightmare lead to the power within?
Do menacing nether waters cover the fish king?

I place the divine fragments into the mandala
Whose centre is the lost creative power.
The sun, the heart of God, the lotus, the electron
The pulse world upon world, ray upon ray
That he who lived on the first may rise on the last day.

-From *Isis Wanderer* by Kathleen Raine

The relationship between Egyptian alchemy and sacred marriage yields rich material focusing on funerary and resurrection mythology. Many eminent theorists, including C. G. Jung, Marie-Louise von Franz, and Edward Edinger, stress the centrality of the Isis-Osiris pairing in the philosophical and physical science of alchemy, as well as within the core psychological understandings of sacred marriage as the *mysterium conjunctionis*.

67 Excerpted from *Regenerating the Feminine: Chronicling Radical Impacts in Psyche, Culture & Nature*, Forthcoming 2021: University Press of Mississippi.

By identifying the roots of alchemy in the fertile loam of the regenerative Nile Valley, depth psychology has developed some of its richest material through the study of Egyptian mythology.

Though often filtered through Greco-Roman classical interpretations, these theories have had continuous impact, informing postmodern culture and psychology. They continue to do so because the integrity of the mythic structure, inherent in the archetypal pairing of the sacrificial year-king with his Sister-Bride, is effective in generating healing as the couple moves *together* through the stages of dismemberment, containment, and resurrection. From its earliest days in Sumer, Babylon, and Crete to the Greco-Roman (partial, incomplete) love goddess-consort incarnations, this ancient partnership lineage forms a foundation for the Christian myth. As such, inquiry into the importance of sacred partnership amplifies the parallels between Isis and Magdalene as Widow-Brides.

Much analysis of the mythology of Isis and Osiris seems to hinge solely on their relationship, principally on Isis' search for her beloved, her labor, and her action towards him. Instead, perhaps Isis and Osiris serve as prototypes of our inner masculine and feminine, simultaneously moving toward *each other* in the radical act of individuation. I suggest that they do so independently, then jointly, and that they can only come together after each has completed his/her respective task. To better understand this rich process requires an examination of three distinct episodes of Egyptian mythology which uniquely inform this psychological alchemy: Isis' securing of the alchemical mystery, the function of Osiris' lead coffin, and their reunion as *conjunctio*.

Isis as Tricky Prophetess

In her investigation of alchemical history/herstory of women alchemists, *Searching for the Soror Mystica: The Lives and Science of Women Alchemists*, Robin Gordon writes that Jung "noticed that the process that an individual undergoes in the course of the individuation journey was mirrored in the alchemical operations" (43). This interpretation of alchemy as metaphor for psychic development correlates alchemical *prima materia* with an undifferentiated (leaden) unconscious and defines psychological development as the personal transformation toward the gold of our differentiating, distilling essence. As such, alchemy becomes a rich, transformative mythological realm.

Marie-Louise von Franz, perhaps the pre-eminent interpreter of Jung, brings much to the discussion of alchemy and her analysis spans several works, flourishing in her landmark book, *Alchemy: An Introduction to the Symbolism and the Psychology*. Though typically referred to as Western medieval studies in the chemical, and sometimes philosophical, transmutation of lead into gold and a search for the elixir of life, the roots of alchemy can be traced to ancient texts and practices arising from various world traditions. While analyzing the amalgamated Hellenic text, *The Prophetess Isis to Her Son*, von Franz explains several essential plot details which show the alchemical value of the myth.[68] She begins with a marginal note in the text—appearing in the same hand as the scribe—which relates that Isis' trip to the town of Hermes is metaphorical, translating as "she means that in a mystical sense" (44). Isis is in the land of the magician, of alchemy, of mystery. The use of the Greek work *kairoi* here describes attending to the astrologically right time. This is significant since, "The alchemist is the [wo/]man who must not only know the technique, but must always consider these constellations" (44). S/he must discriminate and pay attention. And, perhaps most significantly, von Franz links Isis' motivation in putting off the angel who wishes to engage with her sexually, with her desire to strike a bargain with him, "getting the alchemical secret out of him" as only a trickster can (45). She goes on to say that whenever the mystery is told, either from the angel to Isis or from Isis to her son or best friend, the two become

68 See Appendix A for the abridged text cited within *Alchemy*.

one to form a mystical union (46). The text is grammatically ambivalent here, and Horus may also be her best friend or there may be two to whom she may tell the mystery. Then, after several paragraphs, the text identifies Isis as the widow:

> Isis is frequently referred to as the widow in the text and therefore from the very beginning in alchemy the philosopher's stone, the mystery, is called the mystery of the widow, the stone of the widow, or the orphan's stone; there was a connection between the widow and the orphan, but it all points to Isis. (50)

Here, von Franz locates Isis and Egyptian mythology at the core of alchemical lore. Isis' identification as the archetypal widow is very significant as it is the inescapable fate of Sister-Brides within the ancient partnership traditions.

Part of the widow's journey is to develop a transformative and mystical practice of grieving—moving through the grief of one who has lived the *unio mystica* and then resides in the deep grief of the *separatio*. Uniquely, the widow—and here I wonder if we might add the widower, divorcée, and divorcé (regardless of legal marital status)—experiences these acts *in this particular order* on her path, pointing us to the cyclical, regenerative life cycle.

Psychologically we can fall into the trap of believing individuation to be a linear path through the alchemical process, one with a definitive and rewarding "ending." (Perhaps this occurs because we seek relief after such an arduous journey.) Rather, individuation is the spiralic development of a lifetime.

And does the orphan not also follow this archetypal pattern? How interesting that the archetypes of widow and orphan appear in the text together. For what do we know of orphanhood but that, through birth, a child is (hopefully) received into blissful union (as the divine child, the elegant third) and then loses it through the *separatio* of death or abandonment. To be alone, even forgotten, after having known love—to be solely responsible for one's own path—perhaps this too is a prerequisite for individuation.[69]

When first one angel, and then his superior, approaches Isis asking for hasty sexual relations she delays them for she is interested in the alchemical mystery. Delaying him in order to trick the secret out of him, she barters, promising to "give herself to him if he first tells her all he knows about that" (45). "Alchemy was born through Isis' resistance and the fact that she did not cede quickly at least delayed the sexual process, if it did not stop it altogether. We do not know what she did in the end, as she very discreetly won't even tell her own son" (57). This act of attaining the secret "implies we have made great progress, we have got this secret out of the angels, something so immense" that it must remain a sacred mystery (54). "[W]hen Isis succeeds in getting the secret from those angels it is seen as a great achievement... [T]he female element, the feminine principle, gets it from deeper layers and then is the mediator who hands it on to [humanity]" (51). Here von Franz acknowledges Isis' trickster action. Though seemingly passive at first blush, it results in acquiring increased consciousness—quite a radical act. Isis' specific actions in the myth, including right cosmic timing, the archetype of the widow, her trickster skills, and her resistance to hasty sex, are key to her alchemical success.

Lead Containment *or* Osiris was a 12-Stepper

Elaborating on the *conjunctio* as the union of conscious and unconscious attitudes, von Franz points toward the leaden component of Osiris' coffin within the myth:

69 See Carol Pearson's analysis of the archetype of the orphan in *Awakening the Hero Within: Twelve Archetypes to Help Us Find Ourselves and Transform Our World* (San Francisco, 1991), 82-93.

> Seth killed Osiris by first making a leaden coffin and then getting people when drunk at a party to enter it under the pretext of finding out whom it would fit. But when Osiris got into the coffin, Seth promptly put the lid on, covering it with lead, and threw it into the sea. Therefore, it could be said that Osiris was suffocated in lead, so you can think of the tomb of Osiris as a lead coffin, or a coffin sealed up with lead within which lies the dead god, or the divine spirit, in the form assumed in death (84).

Here von Franz describes how Seth and Osiris act out a psychic duel, the dance between our shadow selves and our consciousness. Her amplification of the raw, leaden qualities of the coffin point to containment of the *materia prima*, raw material necessary for alchemical transformation. Stressing the necessity for containment she continues:

> The vessel is a symbol for the attitude which prevents anything escaping outside; it is a basic attitude of introversion which, on principle, does not let anything escape into the outside world. The illusion that the whole trouble lies outside oneself has to come to an end and things have to be looked at from within. That is how we "suffocate" the Mysterium of the unconscious. We do not know what the unconscious is, but we suffocate it through this concentrated treatment by which all projection is stopped, intensifying the psychological process. It is also the torture of fire, because when the flow of intensity of the psychological processes becomes concentrated, one is roasted, roasted in what one is. Therefore, the person in the tomb and the tomb itself are the same thing, for you roast in what you are yourself and not in anything else; or one could say that one is cooked in one's own juice, and is therefore the tomb, the container of the tomb, the suffocated one, and the suffocator, the coffin, and the dead god in it (87).

Here von Franz offers the transformative motif of cooking as it applies to alchemy. She suggests that transformation requires appropriate heat and a beaker/cauldron/container. Containment provides a place for creativity to unfold; to make soup, a pot is required. Von Franz is emphatic that in order to overcome projections we must be somewhat trapped with them to "suffocate" them, an intense form of self-examination. While this might seem to be a simple alchemical step—perhaps one of the most straightforward in the Egyptian myths surrounding Osiris—it is, at least in postmodernity, an exceptional challenge to remain still within (or committed to) our bubbling caldrons, our personal alchemical containers. Similarly, this alchemical step works within seasonal gardening mythology, with the compost bin standing in as transformative container. Without waste, we have no compost.

With our physical and psychic containers having withstood so much harm done through physical, emotional, and sexual abuse, many have cracked and ruptured, some beyond repair. Not only do we leak moist psychic energy and libido (erotic life force as Jung describes it, prana or chi), we are frequently unaware of doing so (unconsciously). We have normalized leakage, creating puddles of projected drama and trauma in our wakes, and the resultant internal desertification and/or flooding of our souls. I suggest this is a tremendous postmodern post-traumatic stress disorder (PTSD), severely hampering healing and our ability to seek support in rebuilding our containers. The subsequent development of addictive behavior in avoidance of *feeling* the resultant deep pain and grief delays the now monumental healing process. Subsequently, it becomes necessary to fight through defensive, destructive armor to reach the root of dis/ease. To feel is to begin to heal. Like Osiris, steeping in his own juices, he is stuck there, with nowhere to run, no way to avoid himself. In order to be resurrected into renewed spiritual life, we must endure that steeping.

Jungian theory and psychotherapy have greatly influenced how addiction is viewed and worked within contemporary Western cultures. Offering a unique synopsis of this phenomenon is Sheri Parks who examines the impact of the dark goddess as "a psychic or spiritual internal presence" (26) in *Fierce Angels: The Strong Black Woman in American Life and Culture*. Especially relevant is her exploration of the significance of the Sacred Dark Feminine, one personification of which is the Black Madonna, perhaps the aspect of the divine feminine most associated with the ancient lineage of Inanna-Isis-Magdalene as Sister-Brides. Parks describes how Jung, "thought the Sacred Dark Feminine to be the oldest archetype. He believed she was so commonly occurring that she was inherited into our collective consciousness—hardwired into our brain chemistry" (5). She writes:

> Jungian therapy holds that one can transcend traumatic circumstances only by facing them. An addict can be cured only after going into the darkness to bottom out. But, according to Jungian therapy, the person is not alone in the darkness, because the Dark Feminine is there with them. She represents endurance and the hope of transformation. She is the guide who will lead the sufferer out, the psychic presence necessary for transformation and a new personal beginning. Jungian therapists and writers routinely use the goddesses and Black Madonnas as references. The popularized version of Jungian therapy is even more far reaching: it is the basis for 12-step programs and all the bestselling self-help books that build upon them. Americans believe in redemption. It is one of the culture's major narratives, and American authors borrow liberally from Jung, who believed that people were always developing and that they could grow out of their past problems; self-help programs and related books borrow directly from Jung to teach us how. Bill Wilson, who cofounded Alcoholics Anonymous, wrote Carl Jung a letter in 1961 to tell him of the organization based on Jungian

> principles. As the basis of AA and the 12-step programs that followed, Jungian therapy has had a tremendous impact on Western culture. The Sacred Dark Feminine has directly or indirectly become part of therapy and self-help of people across the country and around the world. (26)

Here, Parks reveals how powerful the Dark Feminine was to Jung, and how present she is in the collective un/consciousness. By acknowledging the impact Jungian psychology has had on 12-step programs and within the entire genre of self-help psychology, Parks identifies the tremendous value and presence of the Dark Feminine as psychopomp in a modern therapeutic sense. The unique qualities inherent in the Dark Feminine are earned from her own alchemical, individuating journey of endurance and offer hope throughout time spent in cryptic exile. Parks' cultural excavations attribute the accessibility of archetypal understanding to Jung as one of psychology's founding fathers, while naming the Dark Feminine as a primal recovery support. Perhaps it is she who anoints us at the darkest hour.

Depth psychology practices faith in transformation on these underworld journeys. In "Surrendering to Psyche: Depth Psychology, Sacrifice, and Culture," Glen Slater describes how psychic dismemberment, if we can survive it, ultimately leads toward wholeness. Working within Greek mythology, he suggests that when faced with underworld tests and tasks "a psychological dismemberment resembling Dionysian ritual will occur—a chaotic, symptomatic sacrifice that, through courage and perseverance, turns into a rootedness in psychic depth" (186-87). For Slater this rootedness evolves through the depth psychological ritual of tending psychic experiences and feelings. Key to understanding alchemical transformations is the need to turn *toward* feelings and grief—to acknowledge their leaden gifts, to lie within them even, to surrender.

In *The Mystery of the Conjunctio: Alchemical Image of Individuation*, Edward Edinger writes that "very gradually we will collect our scattered psyche from the outer world, as Isis gathered the dismembered body of Osiris, and in doing that we will be working on the conjunctio" (18). He goes on to describe how the sacred or chemical marriage is the culmination of the alchemical process. "According to alchemical symbolism, the *conjunctio* is the goal of the process: It's the entity, the stuff, the substance that is created by the alchemical procedure when finally it succeeds in uniting the opposites" (18). Edinger views the *conjunctio* as the destination of the often long, arduous, and ultimately mysterious journey of individuation. Such expression of union within the psyche is at the heart of the interplay between Isis and Osiris and is possible only after each has done his/her individual work.

Von Franz suggests that the end of an age might be marked by a radical shift in consciousness. It is the end of the Egyptian civilization that amplifies the mythology of Isis, so much so that a rich and extensive "cult" dedicated to her develops throughout the Roman empire; interestingly, this devotion coincides with the shifting of astrological ages from Aries to Pisces. Beliefs exhaust themselves and come to an end, providing space for something new to come into being. In the case of civilizations previously dominated by severe laws, dogma, or rigidly structured social norms, a time generally arises when the pendulum swings to the other side. "[B]ecause these things come to an end, to an enantiodromia, the masculine mode of consciousness tires. That is a typical archetypal event, and then the feminine, or the unconscious and nature, the chaotic, have to take back the light" (62). For von Franz, this movement symbolizes a back and forth between poles. Enantiodromia describes the tendency of something to become its opposite. This rebalancing action evokes pendulum swings, arcs moving from extremity to extremity. Another interpretation might allow for a more integrative and holistic synthesizing, as Isis gathered and re/membered her beloved, as both Isis and Mary Magdalene retrieve, anoint, and tenderly wrap the bodies of their beloved partners with spice and fragrance.[70]

With such a time again upon us—some suggest we are currently shifting astrologically to the Aquarian age—the integrating skills of Isis as priestess of light and darkness might be called upon again. She searches for her entombed beloved, attends the dismembered one, uniting with him as two who have individually labored to become whole. Together they bring forth a new kind (queered, if you will) of wholeness.

Resurrection means change—dramatic, painful, awe/ful change from death—the kind that often renders us unrecognizable, especially to ourselves. Resurrection does not mean returning to life as usual. It is not coming *back* to the life we once had but rather, traveling forward. For Osiris it was *life* in a completely different form. From flesh and blood king he became immortal, a god of the underworld, leaving his body behind. This motif repeats with other sacrificial year-kings, including Dionysus—who shares with Osiris regenerative grain symbolism—and Jesus, who left the Earthly plane for a seat at his father's right hand. I can only imagine a highly charged and animated conversation between these newly resurrected ones, transformed toward a healing masculine.

Excerpt from *Regenerating the Feminine: Chronicling Radical Impacts in Psyche, Culture & Nature*, Forthcoming 2021: University Press of Mississippi.

70 See Margaret Merisante, "Tears and Fragrance for the God's Death and Resurrection: The Funerary Syncretism of Mary Magdalene with Isis" (Unpublished, 2015).

Appendix A

"The Prophetess Isis to Her Son" as told by Marie-Louise von Franz in *Alchemy*

Note: This Greek text from the Hellenic period is perhaps a composite of earlier Egyptian writings with no clear lineage cited. The text is found in the compilation entitled the Codex Marcianus, named for the Mariana library in Venice (see von Franz 41-3). Included here is von Franz's own translation (presumably from the German though nowhere in the book does she cite her source) complete with her bracketed interpretations. The text appears interspersed with her commentary throughout her second lecture on Greek alchemy (44-50) and is missing two pages near the end (indicated here by ...) which she summarizes instead (see pages 47-50). Alternative translations are now readily available online in their entirety.

Oh, my son, when you desired to go away to fight the treacherous Typhon [i.e., Seth] over your father's kingdom [the kingdom of Osiris], I went to Hormanouthi, i.e., Hermoupolis, the town of Hermes, the town of the holy technique of Egypt, and stayed there some time.

After a certain passing of the kairoi and the necessary movement of the heavenly sphere, it happened that one of the angels who dwelt in the first firmament saw me from above and came towards me desiring to unite with me sexually. He was in a great hurry for this to happen, but I did not submit to him. I resisted, for I wished to ask him about the preparation of gold and silver.

When I put my question, he said he did not wish to answer me since it was such a great mystery [the superlatively great mystery —to give a freer translation—because this mystery is too overwhelming], but said he would be able to answer me and solve my problem. And he told me about his sign [meaning probably how she should recognize the angel] and that he would bear on his head, and take it and show me, a ceramic vessel full of shining water. He [the other angel] wanted to tell me the truth. This vessel is a possoton and has no pitch in it.

The next day, when the sun was in the middle of its course [that is, at midday], there came down the angel who was greater than the other, and he was gripped by the same desire of me and was in a great hurry. [He too wanted to rape Isis]. But none the less I only wanted to ask him my question. [She again delays, thinking only of the question.] When he stayed with me, I did not give myself to him. I resisted him and overcame his desire till he showed me the sign on his head, and gave me the tradition of the mysteries without keeping anything back, but in the full truth. [So she wins the battle and he tells her all he knows about the technique of alchemy.] He then again pointed to the sign, the vessel he carried on his head, and began telling the mysteries and about the message. Then he first mentioned the great oath and said: "I conjure you, in the name of Fire, of Water, of Air and of the Earth [twice a quaternio]; I conjure you in the name of the Height of Heaven and the Depth of the Earth and the Underworld; I conjure you in the name of Hermes and Anubis, the Howling of Kerkoros and the guardian dragon; I conjure you, in the name of that boat and its ferryman, Acharontos; and I conjure you in the name of the three necessities, and the whips and the sword." After he had pronounced this oath, he made me with this oath promise never to tell the mystery I was now to hear, except to my son, my child, and my closest friend, so that you are me, and I am you.

Now you go and watch and ask Acheron the peasant. [A variation gives Acharontos. There is no transition here in the text, but probably from now on we hear the mystery. Unfortunately in those days they had no signs, no quotes, or anything like that. One never knows where the quotes should be, but I think it is obvious that it begins here. It means that now the mystery will be imparted and you should listen to it.] Come and look, and ask the peasant Acharontos, and learn from him who is the sower, who is the harvester, and learn that he who sows barley will also harvest barley and he who sows wheat will also harvest wheat. Now my child, or my son, you have heard that as an introduction, and now realize from that that this is the whole creation and the whole process of coming into being, and know that a man is only able to produce a man, and a lion a lion, and a dog a dog, and if something happens contrary to nature [probably meaning contrary to this law], then it is a miracle and cannot continue to exist, because nature enjoys nature, and nature overcomes nature. [That is the famous saying which also appears in many other texts, but usually as: "Nature enjoys nature, nature impregnates nature, and nature overcomes nature."] Having part of the divine power and being happy about its divine presence, I will now also answer their questions about sands, which one does not prepare from other substances, for one must stay with existing nature and the matter one has in hand in order to prepare things. Just as I said before, wheat creates wheat, and a man begets a man, and thus also gold will harvest gold, like produces like. Now I have manifested the mystery to you.

Take quicksilver, fix it in lumps of earth or by magnesia or sulphur and retain it. [This is fixation through warmth, the mixture of species.] Take one part of lead and of the preparation fixed through warmth, and two parts of the white stone, and from the same stone one part, and one part of yellow Realgar [that means red sulphur of arsenic] and one part of the green stone [one does not know what that is]. Mix the whole with lead, and when it has disintegrated, reduce it three times to a liquid [i.e., melt it three times].

Take quicksilver which through copper has become white, and take from it another one part and from dominant magnesia, with one part of water, and with lemon juice, use one part, and from arsenic which has been catalyzed with the urine of a not yet corrupted boy, one part, and then from Cadmeia [cadmia, calamine in English, which simply implies a mineral which engenders fire], one part and one part from sand cooked with sulphur, and from lead monoxide with asbestos two parts, and from the ashes of Kobathia [that is probably also an arsenic sulphite] one part, and liquidate the whole with a very sharp acid, a white acid, and dry it, and then you have the great white remedy.

...

If you want to make something white of the bodies [i.e., the material], mix it with quicksilver and drops of asbestos and urine and goatsmilk and natron, and then you can make everything work, and if you want to know how to double the substance, or how to colour the material, and all the dispositions, then know that everything has the same meaning [and that is important', that everything tends to have the same meaning [i.e., the meaning is likely always to be the same for operation]. Now realize the mystery, my son, the drug, the elixir of the widow.

Take arsenic, cook it in water, mix it with olive oil, and then leave it in a bottle and put coals on it until it steams and also the same thing can be made with Realgar...

"Here the text breaks off, and then is repeated all over again" (50).

Reflection on an Egyptian Goddess

Sharon Smith

Auset, I know your pain.
You lost your Love too...
It changes you, doesn't it?
Here today, gone tomorrow...
Life becomes a dark, shadowed land
and you wander it aimlessly
wanting only to embrace once again
what you have lost.
You know the road of which I speak:
You traveled it across the desert spaces of Egypt yourself
in search of your lost Love.
You found him only to lose him a second time.
I don't envy you that double loss:
once was more than enough for me.
But Love was born of that hallowed space after your losses.
And Love was born from the dark space after my own loss.
Your Love manifested in Horus;
mine in learning to love myself.
But both were acts of Defiance,
of Sovereignty:
Yours toward Set, who robbed you of your Love;
mine toward the Patriarchy,
which robbed me of my Self.
We both stood our ground, didn't we?
We refused to bend, to break,
to give up, to give in...
We both are Dangerous Women
to the men who want to define and control us,
to strip us of our rightful places and our power.
You taught me this:
That the struggle is not a sign of weakness,

but an opportunity to cultivate Courage and Strength,
to rise above it all
and reclaim what is ours.
You showed me, Dear Auset,
that loss does not have to end us:
It can begin us.
And you reminded me
that Goddesses are not seated in exalted heavenly places:
They walk among us,
because they ARE us.

Isis, Mother Goddess of the Universe

Tara Reynolds

The Alchemies of Isis Embodiment

Carmel Glenane

Isis will allow your "soul" to grow through loss and pain and she brings "life" back to you when you are letting go of the past. She waits for you to be ready for her, and she brings patience to you when you are in a space of despair. She allows you to renew yourself through her. Hope, restoration, and magic are yours when you lovingly embrace Isis. She knows the value of balanced passion and she will bring to your life all that you desire to create a mate and keep the fires glowing between you and your beloved.

Isis offers restoration of harmony after losses; she understands loss and tragedy, and the pain of relationship loss. Isis knows how to allow you to really go into the heart of yourself through the grieving process, and then let it go. Isis is ideal for balancing and restoring emotional equilibrium.

Strong, healthy relationships come from yourself and through you. You can really allow the magic of the Alchemies of Isis – The Magician to come to you.

Isis brings now the frequency of truth for all of life in relationship patterning. For your life and world now you are embracing a new way of being human and this is to consider yourself first in everything. Isis creates through balanced love.

Through the essence of balanced, heart-centered love, you can begin to really delve into yourself and ask yourself why you don't consider yourself "first" in everything. For your relationship with The Alchemies of Isis to develop in your consciousness, you must just consider why it is such a challenge to consider YOU in your journey with yourself.

Isis holds the key to the feminine mysteries because she helps you change your relationship with your feminine. Your feminine essence is enacted when you begin to embrace the living energies of Isis, for she is the Great Magician. The embracing of your own sexual powers to heal, renew, and change consciousness belongs to Isis. For Isis heals through the alchemy of the sexual energy.

Isis brings the sexual energy to the frequency of passion that is heart-balanced. She brings the balance back into the rejuvenation qualities sexual passion creates. Sexuality creates rejuvenation. The tissues, cells, and endocrine (hormonal function) are all under Isis protection for she RULES THROUGH THE MOON and the moon's powers belong to her.

You must remember that the feminine arts are the moon's magic. Through the effects of the moon and the water element, the energy of sexuality is brought to the heart to heal and renew. If sexuality is not connected to the heart, it destroys because it burns the essence of the feminine with its power.

ISIS LOVES BEING IN THE COMPANY OF THOSE WHO CAN APPRECIATE AND SUPPORT LOVE. WHERE THERE IS NO UNDERSTANDING OF LOVE OR APPRECIATION OF LOVE AS A WAY OF BEING HUMAN, ISIS CANNOT STAY.

YOU MUST INTONE DAILY:

"I NOW ALLOW MYSELF THE APPRECIATION OF LOVE. THE APPRECIATION OF LOVE MAKES ME WHOLE AND FEEDS MY IMMORTAL SOUL."

ISIS BRINGS YOUR BODY INTO A STATE OF ALIGNMENT WITH YOUR TRUTH. YOUR TRUTH IS A BAROMETER FOR LOVE AND YOUR TRUTH REVEALS LOVE TO YOU IN ITS PUREST FORM.
Isis teaches you to nourish your body and keep it in a state of

renewal, because your relationship with your body is a statement about how you cherish your emotions.

Your emotions reflect your relationship with your body. Your body is a barometer of your emotions and their well-being.

You must just feel the emotional energy and find where in the body emotional energy is held. You must allow yourself this peace, knowing Isis rules the relationship WITH THE BODY AND THE EMOTIONS. THEY ARE NOT SEPARATE.

Find a space within yourself to create with this energy. You must first seek to allow yourself the knowledge that you have a right to begin to create the conditions for your love of the alchemical processes, which give the body vigor, life force, and magnetism.

For the body to have the magnetism to bring power, radiance, and inner beauty, Isis suggests you begin to really allow the body to absorb the energies of nature, especially the natural world, by being near bodies of water where the moon's powers can magnetize water. Taking moon-energized water internally and bathing in moon water brings the magnetic power of renewal to you now.

Why am I Here?

As you take your journey deep into yourself, you are reliving your past and releasing it as well. You are being encouraged now to stop and ponder the meaning of why you are here, and to bathe in the incandescent energy of love all around you. Right now it is important to allow yourself this merging with all selves, which support your journey. To begin to allow the essence, energy, and life force of universal vibrations to assist reinforces your belief in the totality of your many selves. These many "selves" are waiting patiently now to be integrated into a whole. It's rather like a jigsaw puzzle. You are looking at all the disassembled parts. These disassembled parts now need to be put into a complete picture. When you begin to do this you are realizing your whole total self where "you" can merge into light, beauty, and power. Merging into oneness creates a sense of peace, space, and order in your life.

See and take apart your old definition of yourself and reassemble it. Allowing yourself to reassemble and rearrange your missing lost bits takes time and patience. Let's go back to the jigsaw puzzle. The picture is looking good but there is one missing piece. This piece is vital for many other pieces that will be found. When the "lost" piece is discovered, there is a sense of joy and accomplishment. The long lost part of yourself has "come home" so to speak.

The excitement and joy of finding this lost part of yourself only reinforces your belief in all your parts being available to be found. As humans, we are like this. We are assembling and looking for the missing "bits" to make the picture "whole." What piece do you need to find today?

Excerpt from: *The Alchemies of Isis Embodiment through The High Priestess* – Carmel Glenane BA Dip Ed ©2015.

Giver of Life

Arna Baartz

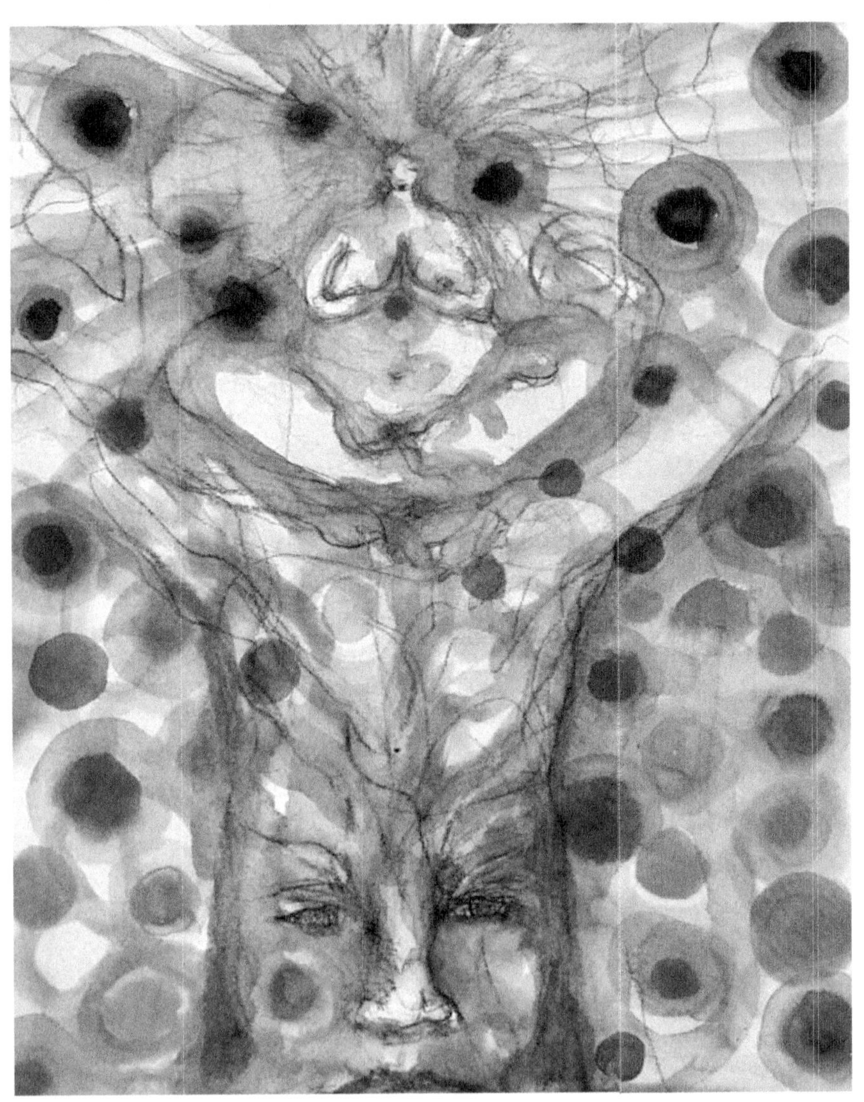

Illustration from *My Name is Isis* by Susan Morgaine.

Weaving

M^h

The story of my life is unravelling before me,
No premeditated form for me to mould myself unto

Blank canvases await the swirls of my sweat and blood

The fight of forgetting who I never was,
A flight to a freedom found in the cosmos that is me

I may have not known of such a possibility before

Never heard of realms where it is not squeezed out of me;
This life force

Always falling short,
In strife I was to trust

But the story of my life is unravelling before me,
I learn to inhale and exhale as an infant just born
Crying to the tune of holding space for myself by being held,
It is not pain, but relief,
A safety just for me
Fashioned to my very needs,
Wounds I now know with certainty will heal,
A quenchless yearning turns to a realised desire
In finding words long searched for –

In a creation tailored to my own flourishing cells

When I need reminders I create my shrine,
Bathing in reviving ritual
Fertility for my dreams and existence fully embodied

A throne of exploration and the ecstatic heights of knowing aliveness
Intimate wings that always lead to familiar safety at the crux of my home,
My body

She reminds me of the she I am, I was and always will be

To walk right into the dark
And entice myself out, bring it all to the surface
To be seen,
A heavy truth is lifted,
Gifted to my inner child,
Devoted to the future that lives and breathes in me

A web of my own energy where none possesses me but me
Spinning nets of nights spent basking in the glow of a waxing moon,
A love fest in the making, solely for one

Not a trap down the way of disenchantment, but self-trust

Unfiltered sands of truth are told,
I take myself back

Oh the sheer pleasure,
In realising-

The magic is me,
The life I seek and have long hidden from is within.

The Gifts of Isis

Talia Segal

I am the last follower of Isis in Her time. I leave this letter to future generations in the hope that what She represents will not be lost hundreds of years from now, even thousands. In the far off time of 900, 1000, even 2000 CE, I hope there exists the Spirit of Isis and all that she gave to the world.

The first gift was Love. Love for Her parents, Her siblings, and the world, newly created. Love for the man who treated Her with respect, kindness, and pride in her abilities.

If Justice is a fruit, the seeds of that fruit are Love. And so through one gift, Isis gave us two.

Justice flowed strong and clear when Isis was our Queen. The people were equals to one another, and love wasn't rare and cherished, the way it is now. And so Her world was broken through an evil act, and Isis was afraid. She followed Her love and gave us the gift of Courage – of acting out of love even when we are afraid.

Courage is a heavy pail of water that gets lighter every time you lift it. If the water of your pail – the love you carry – is shared amongst your neighbors, so much the better.

Isis left her position of privilege and searched the world for Her partner. She took Her disguise not from rulers but from the people. As an old woman was She able to find her Love. Shouldering the hard work of caring for children, She located Her husband – dead – inside a tree. And from Her refusal to be defeated do we receive Her gift of Hope.

Isis took Hope and Courage and Justice and Love, wrapped Her arms around Osiris, and brought Him back to life.

O Isis, it was then that you had me. Your wings encircled Your King, and Your power flowed through You both. In that moment, I found something that changed me forever. With Your gift of Magic, the world was never the same.

Reader, I cannot speak to you about the gifts She gave to Her followers during our sacred rites. Those remain a secret I hold close to my heart.

But Love, Justice, Courage, Hope, and Magic are what sustain us all, and I fear we won't survive without them.

If the night wasn't so black, the stars wouldn't be visible. Isis is both the dark and the bright. Together. Whole.

So this letter I write to you, Queen, Goddess, Witch of the future. That you may know the Truth: All answers lie within you. You have everything you need.

I am Isis

Kat Shaw

I am Isis.
Creator, Mother, Healer.
The wisdom of the entire universe.
Proud, Independent. Powerful.
Dignified and elegant.
Goddess of life.
Goddess of fertility.
Goddess of motherhood.
Protector of women and children.
Giver of life.
Queen of the throne.
I am pure magic.

Awakening Your Voice with Isis

Dominique Oyston

To be seen, heard and valued are fundamental human needs. We all hunger to express the truth of our nature and the essence of our existence.

Your voice is the primary tool by which you deliver and share who you are. Everything you are comes through your voice: your uniqueness, your personality, your message and your mission. What happens in your throat centre impacts who you are and everything you experience. The light of Isis can support your voice to grow, fully flower and become a useful tool that you can use to flourish in your life or business.

I am a professional opera singer, intuitive and voice expert who founded an online business called The Goddess Voice Academy. I teach voice for speaking, performance, personal confidence, sound healing and to guide women to embody their full spiritual and physical expression.

During my 25 years travelling the world as a singer, I studied mythology, the mysteries of the ancient cultures, the spiritual teachings of sound and many healing modalities.

I knew that the voice was a primary vehicle for spiritual development and earthly manifesting, and I followed the call to understand this as deeply as I could. Your voice is a mighty conduit between your human and divine natures – but 3,000 years ago, when women were banished from the public speaking sphere and visible positions of authority – it totally changed the course of our understanding of the power of the voice.

People are no longer confident with their full, natural voice because the feminine aspects have been shamed. They have been sidelined and subdued into silence and servility by patriarchy, cast out from our bodies and become hidden deep down. The secrets and deeper wisdom of the voice as a tool of transformation and healing have been devalued and lost.

But we are awakening, and this story is about how the goddess Isis showed me steps to reclaiming the sovereignty of the feminine within my voice. Calling the light of Isis into my voice broke through blocks to the place of intense truth in my personal life and empowered me to speak that truth. Isis showed me how to balance the masculine and feminine aspects of my voice to transform my wounded relationship. And as I worked with her light, I came out of the spiritual closet to finally feel comfortable to be professionally seen and heard as 'magical.'

I would love to share how to awaken her light within your voice too.

The Voice of the Goddess

Isis was considered more powerful than a thousand soldiers and 'the clever-tongued one whose speech never fails.' She was the teacher of voice magic and connected to the lineage of Hathor, 'She of a Thousand Voices.' She spoke words of power to shapeshift reality and to bring physical healing, balance, love and divine truth back to the world.

The various spiritual tasks of the voice were well-practiced in ancient cultures and they formed the basis of many healing centres across the globe. Sound healing and using the voice as medicine and alchemy were fundamental in Egypt until they were lost to mainstream consciousness with the rise of the Roman Catholic Church. The Romans were conquerors and did not care for that much autonomy and healing wisdom to be in the hands of the worshippers of the old gods and goddesses.

Isis reminds us that many of us were connected to the magical voice in Egypt. You were a healer and wisdom keeper. You were warmed by the sun and the great river. Your magic re-awakens with Isis. You too can speak the words of power once more.

Equality of Masculine and Feminine

Isis was equal with her husband. One was not superior to the other. They created together in harmony and she showed me how the best voices are a blending of masculine and feminine qualities. Revealing your spiritual gifts and bringing them to the voice, is an act of masculine assertiveness, supported by the feminine field of wisdom, flow and nurturing. Our inner SHE loves, soothes, grounds and provides the intuitive, fertile wisdom for our inner HE to express and take action.

This merger generates a powerful rulership energy. It decreases stage fright and fear of public speaking and assists with the process of communicating with balance. It resolves procrastination so you can birth your creative dreams and projects. Mother and father will create a child.

Remembering Your Voice

The role of the divine feminine voice and the wisdom of the mystery schools is being collectively remembered at this point in time. Women have suffered over the centuries and it takes a quest to uncover your unique voice wisdom that has vanished or been made 'less than.'

Ask, and Isis can awaken your voice of sacred service.

Your journey will include longing, confusion and searching to learn how to use your voice for its sacred and powerful purpose. If you are not sure where to start, begin by feeling into the thing that you 'secretly' want to do with your voice.

What draws you the most? Is it:

- Sharing the thing that feeds your soul
- Being on stage as a singer or speaker
- Light language or chant
- Working with vibrations and harmonies
- Prayer, blessing and invocation
- Using your voice for a specific purpose
- Healing nature, yourself or others
- Unleashing light and power in the form of words, inspiration or poetry
- Guiding, teaching or supporting others
- Seeing, hearing and channeling Spirit
- Priestessing with your voice
- Walking toward spiritual leadership

You may not quite know yet. It's common to feel connected to these things as a child or teenager but then spend years trying to figure out what it means. Rise to the call of your voice.

The Gift within Your Voice

Your soul gifts exist in the quantum field and finding your voice helps you manifest them. Everyone has a gift in their voice. Your gift may be lying dormant within you, untouched through lifetimes or it may carry trauma and have shrunk into its shell for refuge. You may have learned not to value your gift as it is not obviously 'useful' or important. But it is there.

What would you feel if people regularly said *"I loved speaking with you, it was pure magic. Thank you so much for sharing and unlocking something I knew I had inside of me."?* How much joy and validation would you receive if people shared "your voice opened my heart."

Lost Voices of the Divine Feminine

Isis is a powerful goddess guide to support you in birthing your divine feminine voice. As you read the following list think of how much scope and authority might be waiting in your throat centre to be reborn. Imagine what it would be like to have one of these voices sitting richly resonant and fully energised inside your body.

- The wisdom voice
- The creative voice
- The intuitive voice
- The healing voice
- The leadership voice
- The pleasure voice
- The magical voice
- The emotional voice
- The womb voice
- The wild woman voice
- The body and embodied voice
- The mother love voice
- The lover's voice
- The priestess voice
- The warrior goddess voice
- The Enchantress
- The Great Mother voice
- The Muse
- The Oracle

- The Siren
- The Songline singer[71]
- The Medicine Woman
- The Shaman

Life changes when we express our value, presence and potency in the public sphere or in our personal life. If you long to use your voice to heal, intuit or speak don't doubt yourself. Have confidence that there is a feminine awakening in your voice as well as your life. You can build a bridge between the ancient wisdom and modern expression to experience the voice that is waiting inside you.

The Mysteries of Sound

If you love Isis you may know that in her temples, the priestesses had very specific voice tasks. Isis was a powerful teacher of the mysteries of sound. The power of language, voice magic, invocation, en'chanting,' healing, light language, bringing through information in the form of sound codes, chant, inspiration, manifesting, poetry, spiritual leadership, guidance, intuition and voice artistry all belong to the voice of Isis. And they belong to you.

Before the goddess spoke, she sang. She knows the birthing, creative mysteries of the body, and she knows the birthing and healing powers of sound, especially song. She deepens your ability to connect to higher dimensions through the arts of singing, toning and sounding.

---

71 The Songlines are a way of describing the Australian Aboroginies 'dreaming' tracks across the land – they sing them to feel them and find their way. We would call them leylines. You can replace this with Leyline singer if you like, but I'd like to keep it in because nomadic people would sing their way across the landscape and the landscape had songs of place.

The Benefits of Finding your Divine Feminine Voice

Tuning in to the goddess light to use your voice in these ways raises your vibration and it raises your IQ. It connects you to the sounds of all creation. It takes you down pathways of imaginative, intuitive and inspirational thinking and academic research. It builds neural pathways between both hemispheres of the brain to enhance creative flow.

Use your divine feminine voice to:

- Purify, clean and tune the chakras and learn sonorous massage
- Connect you to your spirituality and your lineage
- Balance your body and emotions
- Restructure your mental field and your brainwaves
- Perform rituals and hold circles
- Give you a greater sense of identity
- Play – the inner child loves sounding
- Trust and know yourself
- Lower blood pressure and activate your immune system
- Recharge your cerebral cortex and stimulate endorphins
- Enhance awareness, bring peace and soothe anxiety
- Stimulate the memory of your higher purpose
- Strengthen the voice-ear connection
- Dissolve fears and boundaries
- Call down spiritual frequencies and birth them through the voice into earthly manifestation
- Heal and sing the world back into wholeness
- Give intuitive guidance and inspiration
- Use words of power and toning to activate consciousness and awaken the truth

If you liberate the voice, you liberate the human being.

If you heal the voice, you heal the human being.

Meditation with the Goddess Isis

I will share a meditation journey I experienced with Isis' light. Emerging from a meditation journey with Isis feels like 20 minutes but most are over an hour and a half. Time stands still.

When Isis moves into my body it is immediately extraordinary, intense and very sensory. She circulates electrical, magnetic currents of light through me. It seems some sort of signature brilliance that her energy carries. Circling through my inner thighs, my lower body, my heart, opening my chest, circling my breasts, opening my throat, opening and circulating an incredible light. Rivers of goddess light running through. Isis is one of the great creator beings of the earth.

I asked what is your 'mission'?

I tried to clear my mind so that my own projections didn't interfere, and I could listen to her rather than interpret.

The words came through – Isis is pure LOVE as creative energy in action through the body temple. She tunes your body, as the house of spirit, to love and complete union in every way between masculine and feminine.

She spoke:

Let me show you how to be divine.
Let me show you how to illumine with light.
Let me show you how to procreate with divinity.

Your breasts are to nourish creation. Your vagina is to receive creation from the masculine impulse of explosive light.

Your womb space is to house, heal and gestate the new form of divine light from that union of pure love.

She showed me how in Egypt many rituals prepared the body with divine light to be the house of the soul; irradiating it with spiritual frequencies, shaping the body with light, healing the body, bringing magic to the body, the magic of divinity, programming and building light into the physical. The priests and priestesses worked to create the sacred union of light and matter to birth the new. They used their voices to do this.

We moved through the body and she shared differently in each area.

Each zone offered a completely alternate use of divine light. Each zone exhibited a different purpose and consequently needed a different frequency.

She was very clear about the vibration for the throat centre.

She spoke:

I am truth, the truth that creates form and relationship.
Truth must be sought in order to find the balance between the masculine and feminine, both inner and outer.

Truth is often personal or subjective. Isis was showing me that to become truly free we must attempt to become aware and honest about how our truth is moving through to our voice. What do we say? How do we say it? What is coming into form through our words and sounds?

Truth is simple. It lives in the throat centre because it is a creative manifesting force that seeks to come into form. It arises spontaneously to be voiced and come into existence. You block truth and try to control it so you can be more comfortable. I don't want 'that' truth, I want 'this' one. When you try to control truth then you are not free.

Isis was one of the creator gods who sang the human body into form and it has been sung in through truth. That is why lie detectors work. Human beings are built upon the laws of spiritual and earthly truth. When we try to control what is true for us and around us to be more comfortable and avoid realities we do not want to face, we are not free. And our voice weakens.

It was a true ancient Egyptian Alchemy meditation. Very physical. Very embodied. Streaming the soul light into the body temple.

Often, I become restless in meditation, but not with Isis' alchemy of voice, body, frequency, light and magic.

Sounding Gratitude

The voice of Isis, High Priestess of the Nile is returning to Earth. You can connect to her by becoming deeply truthful in everything you say and acknowledging that truth is a creative force.

Feel her wings enfold you and know you are safe to express.

Let the limitless light she offers be a bridge to unlock the light of your own communication.

She is mother and loving partner, co-creator of the path of balance between sun and moon, heaven and earth.

Sound with her and you sound your own rebirth.

In Egypt, Ong is the form of Om. Sing with Isis a song of gratitude, a song of truth.

Finding Your Frequency

Your quest to rediscover your feminine soul will include an adventure to reclaim your authentic voice. Your soul song and your frequency are like homing beacons calling your destiny to you.

Imagine now that your voice is rising up within you. You are alive with sound. You're free to speak your truth; singing, chanting, acting, toning, poetry, oratory, laughter, giving awesome advice, FB Lives, videos, speeches, delivering your message freely and healing. You allow yourself to drop into your full physical resonance with peace and trust. You let your voice step out from its usual pathways and speak differently. You understand and direct the vibrations that come through.

Your voice is your birthright. Let it rise.

Goddess be.

Isis

Sudie Rakusin

Taking Your Throne[72]

Syma Kharal

> Mighty one,
> foremost of the Goddesses
> Ruler in heaven,
> Queen on earth...
> All the deities
> are under Her command.
>
> —Inscription to Isis at Philae

My beloved, here you are. Here you are. Awakened to your feminine wisdom and power by the grace of all the Goddesses you have activated within you on this journey.

It is time now, my sister, to take your rightful throne so that you may sit as the Sovereign Queen in the center of your life.

Initiating you on your final, most blessed step is the Queen Goddess of all Herself, the adored and venerated Egyptian Goddess Isis. Her Kemetic (ancient Egyptian) name *Auset* or *Ast* means "throne," and Her hieroglyphic sign is also the throne, for She is ruler of all Gods and Goddesses in heaven and of all kings and queens on earth. She is the very personification of the Divine and regal power of the throne.

Beyond the throne, as Goddess of Ten Thousand names, Isis is the culmination and embodiment of *all Sacred Feminine powers* you have awakened on your journey thus far, and all that you ever will

72 This chapter is from Syma Kharal's book, *Goddess Reclaimed: 13 Initiations to Unleash Your Sacred Feminine Power*, which thoroughly discusses 13 Goddesses and culminates with an extensive chapter on Isis. To compliment the flow of this anthology, we chose to break the chapter up into 4 parts.

after. As Isis-Panthea, She is the "All Goddess," the fullest expression of your Divine nature alchemized and actualized. She is here to remind you that it is time to take the lead in your life and become an empowered, wise, abundant, and loving Queen in your domain and in the world. She is here to show you that as Goddess of all Goddesses, She is *all of you*: dark and light, human and Divine, woman and Goddess.

Her all-encompassing nature is expressed through Her countless names, hymns inscribed on Her sacred temples, and ancient texts that have been translated by devotees and scholars alike for thousands of years. The truth of Her sacred words has the power to awaken and affirm your own nature as Queen Goddess of all, and I hope as you read the passages below that they do.

For when you know yourself as Isis, you are in essence simultaneously invoking all the Goddesses you have met individually. You are weaving all their gifts within the tapestry of your own essence, consciously embodying and expressing the full spectrum of your Divine Feminine nature.

Isis as Goddess of Silence

One of Isis's names in the Egyptian *Book of the Dead* is "Lover of silence."[73] Like Sige, She is also associated with the Goddess of knowledge and wisdom, Sophia, and in this form She is even called Isis-Sophia.

In "The Thunder, Perfect Mind," a Coptic text incorporated into the Gnostic *Nag Hammadi*, Isis-Sophia affirms Herself as "the silence that is incomprehensible and the idea whose remembrance is frequent."[74]

---

73 E.A. Wallis Budge, *The Book of the Dead*, (Publication of 1895 based on the *Papyrus of Ani* in possession of the British Museum) 1895.

74 George W. MacRae, "The Thunder, Perfect Mind," *Nag Hammadi*, Codex VI, Tractate 2: Protocol of the Fifth Colloquy (1973) The Center for Hermeneuti-

Isis is the empty presence through which you will continue to receive, conceive, and birth your Divine wisdom as you move forward. She is the idea of your own Divine self whose remembrance is as frequent as you connect with it in sacred stillness.

She is the voice of the soul of the universe speaking through your own soul, through outer signs and inner guidance. She is the word of the Divine and of truth, which appears to you in endless ways, so that you may connect in ways that most speak to *your* soul.

Isis is the sacred mystery that is accessible to us all. She is the guidance that is to be felt through the heart and known through the soul, which cannot be comprehended through the mind alone.

As ancient Greek high priest and scribe Plutarch shared with a priestess of Delphi (first century AD), Isis "discloses the Divine mysteries to those who truly and justly have the name of 'bearers of the sacred vessels' and 'wearers of the sacred robes.'"[75]

When you robe yourself in solitude and silence the voice in your mind, you open the chambers of your soul, inviting Divine wisdom to enter and fill you. You become, as a High Priestess, the vessel for the Goddess to flow through you.

Isis, like Sige, is the essence of silence, and the great void through which all is birthed. She gently implores you to access Her wisdom through a conscious, daily practice of stillness. For only in silence can She speak to you clearly. And only in stillness can you perceive Her mysteries.

---

cal Studies in Hellenistic and Modern Culture, 1975.

75 Plutarch, *Moralia*, vol. 5, trans. Frank Cole Babbitt (Loeb Classical Library edition, 1936).

Isis as the Goddess of Heaven and the Underworld

Isis is also here to solidify your initiation with the next Goddesses you met after Sige, for She is Queen of heaven, earth, and the underworld. As She proclaims to Her devotee Lucius in his tale, *The Metamorphosis*, Isis is "the sovereign of the spirits of the dead, the first of the celestials."[76]

She is the one who rules "the luminous summits of the heavens, the salubrious breezes of the sea, and the deplorable silences of the realms beneath."[77]

She is your spirit and your shadow, your human grief and your Divine power. She needs you to see your light and dark. For Isis knows the pangs of grief and is a Goddess of mourning and lamentation Herself. Like Ereshkigal who bit Her lip and slapped Her thigh when Inanna entered Her domain, Isis cut Her hair and tore Her clothes when She heard of Her beloved husband Osiris's death by Their jealous brother Set.

In the *Egyptian Book of the Dead*, it is said that when She set out to search for His body, Isis "wandered round and round the earth uttering cries of pain, and She rested not until She had found Him." Her tears flooded the Nile every spring, inundating and fertilizing the desert lands to create new life from death, as Inanna arose anew from Hers. Both Goddess myths of descending into the underworld and ascending into new life honor the cycles of death, healing, resurrection, and renewal that we too are initiated into through the seasons of our lives and in our very own cyclical nature as women. Isis is the power to be found through the wisdom in your wounds. And She asks once again that you embrace and not forsake their gifts, beloved. She wants you to take your throne as you delve below into

76 Apuleius, *The Metamorphosis, or The Golden Ass, and Philosophical Works of Apuleius*, trans. Thomas Taylor (London: Sold by R. Triphook and T. Rodd, 1822).

77 Ibid.

Ereshkigal, Queen of the underworld (your unconscious, shadow self), and revere Her equally as you come up to sit on your heavenly throne (your conscious, spiritual self) as Inanna. Only then can you be the rightful ruler of your whole self.

Isis as the Goddess of Transformation

Isis, as Lady of heat and fire and Lady of lightning, comes to you next as the lava fires of Pele's wrath, which will continue to erupt when rightfully called for. For She is both the "control and the uncontrollable" and the "union and the dissolution."[78]

She is the Divine Feminine *shakti* within you that is yours to wield at your will—to unleash for destruction of the old and creation of the new.

Just as Pele is the Goddess of unrestrained forces like lava and lightning, Isis is the unbridled harbinger of transformation. In addition to being the Mistress of all elements, Isis has powerful tools at Her disposal to shake up old foundations, one of which was Her magical *sistrum* (ancient Egyptian rattle). As Plutarch shares, "The sistrum also makes it clear that all things in existence need to be shaken, or rattled about, and never to cease from motion but, as it were, to be waked up and agitated when they grow drowsy and torpid."

Like Pele's erupting volcanoes, Isis knows that sometimes unleashing disruptive forces is the only way to clear what no longer serves you and fertilize the lava-enriched soils for new beginnings.

---

78 George W. MacRae, "The Thunder, Perfect Mind," *Nag Hammadi*, Codex VI, Tractate 2: Protocol of the Fifth Colloquy (1973) The Center for Hermeneutical Studies in Hellenistic and Modern Culture, 1975.

Both Goddesses invite you to own your sacred rage as you move forward so that you may cleanse your life and clear the way, dancing like Pele and Isis in rapture and with abandon.

Isis as the Goddess of Power

Isis now affirms your inner Kali, to continue to liberate and empower you. Her names as the Mighty One, Protectress, Savioress, and Goddess of war are your own Divine powers to overcome your greatest inner and outer foes.

While men have long been ascribed the role of protector, Isis reminds women that we hold the power to protect ourselves, our children, and our men. In the *Book of the Dead*, She is credited for Her role in protecting not only Her son Horus as a single mother, but even Her God-king husband Osiris: "Thy sister put forth Her protecting power for thee, She scattered abroad those who were Her enemies."

Like Kali *Ma*, Isis is the fiercely protective Mother, for She had to protect Her son Horus from Her brother Set, who sought to murder the holy child as He did Osiris. She went through many harsh trials of Her own, each one testing the bounds of Her strength. But as She always persevered, each test elevated Isis to a new level of Her own Divine strength, wisdom, and power.
As one who has transcended tragedy and trial, Isis knows the necessity of harsh transformation. She reminds you that whatever trials life sends your way, know that each one is an invitation to a higher initiation on your spiritual path. For only in the taking away and tearing down of all that you hold dear can you come to know your true self. No matter how much you resist, She will sever all your attachments to align you back with your truth out of Her love for you. You can count on it.

And yet, Isis knows what it is like to be afraid in the face of adversity, for She is the one who "exists in all fears and (is) strength in trembling."[79] As you tremble with fear when facing the obstacles before you or demons within you, Isis as Kali is your own inner Warrioress, summoning your bloodlust and screaming out your battle-cry to overcome all that stands in the way of your liberation and highest self-realization.

Isis as the Goddess of Compassion

And when you are done with your battling and just need a soft place to fall, Isis is Kuan Yin as the Sacred Feminine gift of compassion within you, just as She appears to the desperate character Lucius in his moment of crisis, lovingly assuring him: "Behold, Lucius, I, moved by thy tears, am present with thee (. . .) I, commiserating thy calamities, I am present, favoring and propitious. Dismiss now your tears and lamentations, and expel sorrow. Now, through my providence, the salutary day will shine upon thee."[80]

Like Kuan Yin, Isis is She who hears all prayers, here to remind you that you are never alone in your suffering, beloved. She reminds you that as Sovereign Queen, you will lead with grace in the world when you offer the grace of compassion to yourself and call in Divine support through your heart-prayers. Isis knows the pains of healing, and like Kuan Yin with Her *amrita* waters, Isis cleanses your heart with Her holy Nile waters. She knows it is the waters of your tears (like Her own) that will revive your soul and spring forth new sprouts of love and blessings in your life.

---

79 George W. MacRae, "The Thunder, Perfect Mind," *Nag Hammadi*, Codex VI, Tractate 2: Protocol of the Fifth Colloquy (1973) The Center for Hermeneutical Studies in Hellenistic and Modern Culture, 1975.

80 Apuleius, *The Metamorphosis, or The Golden Ass, and Philosophical Works of Apuleius*, trans. Thomas Taylor (London: Sold by R. Triphook and T. Rodd, 1822).

Isis as the Goddess of Love

Love, too, is Isis's domain, for She herself says to Lucius, "on Cyprus they call me golden Aphrodite."[81]

As Aphrodite within you, She is the source of Divine love, radiant beauty, sacred sexuality, and ecstatic pleasure. And She knows the price we women pay as we dare to embrace these gifts as She herself has been called both "the whore and the holy one."[82]

Isis as your inner Aphrodite sweetly beckons you to love your body and honor your soul so that you may be the holy vessel of endless pleasures, merging all the delights of heaven and earth through your beautiful body temple. She reminds you that you are both sexual and sacred, and you have a sovereign right to experience yourself as both.

Her names attribute Her as simultaneously being the Divine Wife and the Great Virgin. Isis is you as the lover who embraces sacred sexual union. She is the devoted and loyal wife/partner who allows Herself to be cherished and ravished by Her beloved. And She is also your self-sufficiency and wholeness, which is yours independent of your relationships.

As Queen-Goddess wife to King-God Osiris, who miraculously conceived their holy child Horus, Isis's union with Her beloved also represents the inner mystical marriage of God-Goddess, and the miracles you birth forth from this. When you love and embrace all of yourself, you unite yourself into sacred wholeness and become the vessel for birthing the Divine through you on earth.

---

81 Ibid.

82 George W. MacRae, "The Thunder, Perfect Mind," *Nag Hammadi*, Codex VI, Tractate 2: Protocol of the Fifth Colloquy (1973) The Center for Hermeneutical Studies in Hellenistic and Modern Culture, 1975.

Aphrodite too birthed Her holy child, Eros, god of romantic love, through Her union with Ares, Her Divine Masculine counterpart. When you merge all the polarities within yourself, their sacred union creates miraculous new expressions of Divine love, within and without.

And you, as a woman, as a Goddess, are the Divine Feminine vessel required for the Divine Masculine (consciousness) to manifest into form. *You* are the Goddess of love. And love begets miraculous creations.

Love as Expressed Through Beauty

Love is beautiful, and as a Goddess, you are the embodiment and bringer of beauty. Isis as Lady of love and Lady of beauty taught women many spiritual and earthly arts, one of which was beautification. In Her colored hieroglyphics (that I was blessed to see for myself during a trip to Egypt), seeing Isis adorned with beautiful makeup, regal clothing, and exquisite jewels is a vision to behold. She is, after all, the Queen Goddess within who compels us to treat ourselves as the worthy and beautiful empresses that we truly are.

For us sensitive, soulful women, it can be easy to invest our time and energy in our spirits. But Isis and Aphrodite remind you that your body is the temple of your spirit. And just as their temples were made and cared for with deep love, reverence, and beauty, they compel you to treat your body the same way. Let this aspect of your inner Isis and Aphrodite empower you to pamper and beautify yourself with joy and without guilt.

These Goddesses also inspire you to bring more beauty into your outer world. Whether it is through fresh flowers, a work of art, sensuous fabrics, magical crystals, or scented candles, take time to delight your senses and your soul through the Sacred Feminine gift of beauty.

Love as the Ultimate Healer

Isis knows and shows that love is the most healing and powerful force of all. Isis searched far and wide across foreign lands to find the body of Her beloved Osiris after Set murdered Him. When Set learned that Isis had found the coffin containing Osiris's body, He repossessed it and then severed the body into fourteen pieces, scattering the late king's dismembered parts into the Nile.
Isis, with the help of Her sister (and wife of Set) Nephthys, once again embarked on a treacherous search for Osiris's body parts.

Through loving determination, They retrieved and tied back together all but one piece: His penis, which was eaten by a fish. Never one to be deterred, Isis fashioned a sacred new phallus for Her beloved out of pure gold. She then began to fervently chant spells and dance around His body so vigorously that Her arms spread into wings, and their beating breathed life back into Osiris. As shared in *The Book of the Dead*, Isis "overshadowed Him with Her feathers, She made wind with Her wings, and She uttered cries at the burial of Her brother."

The revival was short-lived but lasted just long enough for the Divine couple to make love one last time. Through the magic of Her love, Isis, "raised up the prostrate form of Him whose heart was still, She took from Him of His essence, She conceived and brought forth a child."[83] Through this final union, Isis miraculously conceived Their son Horus, who would go on to avenge His father, restore Isis upon Her throne, and become the just and rightful king of Upper and Lower Egypt.

Like Isis, Aphrodite too lost her beloved Adonis when he pursued a dangerous hunt after the Goddess's pleas for him not to, and he was tragically killed by a wild boar. As Aphrodite held Her deceased lover in Her arms, in Her mourning, She turned the

---

83 E.A. Wallis Budge, *The Book of the Dead*, (Publication of 1895 based on the *Papyrus of Ani* in possession of the British Museum) 1895.

blood that dripped from his lifeless body into bright red anemone flowers.

Both Goddesses remind us that through the power of love, even the deepest heartbreak can be healed, and the greatest tragedies can be transformed. This alchemical elixir is the endless source of Divine love within you, beloved. You can always draw on it for your own restoration and renewal, no matter what your heart goes through as you open it to the joys and pains of loving.

Isis as the Goddess of Wishes

Isis is also your highest hopes and dreams, as is the wish-fulfilling Tara. Her names Isis-Sothis and Isis-Sopdet connected the Goddess to the star we know as Sirius and in which form She was depicted with a star upon Her crown. The resurgence of Sirius in the spring marked the inundation of the Nile and beginning of a new year, one pregnant with renewed hope and promise.

Just as Tara inspired you with Divine visions for your soul's dreams, Isis invites you to align your hopes with the brightest of all the stars: Sirius. She is the light of your heart's highest aspirations. She is the brilliance of your soul's greatest expression. Whenever you set standards for your life and affirm your Divine dreams, shoot for nothing less than the brightest of all of heaven's stars as is befitting for the Queen that you are.

And, like Tara, Isis offers you Her complete protection as you shine your brightest light and live your most glorious life. She says as much to you as She did to Lucius, "You will live happy, you will live glorious, under my protection."[84]

---

84 Apuleius, *The Metamorphosis, or The Golden Ass, and Philosophical Works of Apuleius*, trans. Thomas Taylor (London: Sold by R. Triphook and T. Rodd, 1822).

Isis as the Goddess of Wisdom

To help you take inspired action to co-create your starry dreams into earthly manifestation, Isis will guide you as your inner wisdom, as your inner Athena. Plutarch described Isis as "a Goddess exceptionally wise and a lover of wisdom, to whom, as Her name at least seems to indicate, knowledge and understanding are in the highest degree appropriate."[85]

Isis, like Athena, gave Her people the practical tools for agriculture, civilization, law and order, commerce, language, and seamanship. Her many attributes connecting Her to Athena are expressed in Her names as Queen of seamanship, justice, lawmaker, knowledge, wisdom, understanding, inventor, Goddess of literature, Goddess of women, Lady of the weaving, and Lady of peace, to name just a few.

Isis is as much a Goddess of esoteric knowledge and magic as She is a patron of strategic planning and practical action. For She knows firsthand that a powerful Queen has to be both. To ensure that you succeed in all your inspired endeavors, Isis as your inner Athena will lovingly encourage you to trust and follow your intuition with joyful, focused, and disciplined action.

She knows that as a woman, you may seek and consider the guidance of those you respect. But She reminds you that while a Queen may have many advisers, ultimately she must seek no council outside of herself when making her decisions and honoring her path.

Isis as the Goddess of Freedom

To keep you soaring high and free on your path, Isis will give you wings as Lilith did in your initiation with Her. She knows

85 Plutarch, *Moralia*, vol. 5, trans. Frank Cole Babbitt (Loeb Classical Library edition, 1936).

and proudly accepts the consequences of being the Wild Woman who is scorned and shunned for honoring Her deepest desires. She proclaims Herself as the one who is both lust and self-control, sinless and the source of sin, and both scorned and venerated.[86]

Isis enchants you into living with sacred lust for life—from the *shakti* fire that erupts from your holy loins. Be the Queen that lives fully and truly. Pay no heed to those who may judge or condemn you. For Isis reminds you that the true sin is self-denial and the greatest punishment is self-betrayal. So spread your wings and fly high, inspiring others to join you if they wish.

Isis also compels you to speak your truth with conviction so that you may honor your values and command the respect you deserve as a woman, as a Queen, and as a Goddess. As She is credited in the *Book of the Dead*, Isis could dispatch those who sought to wrong Her through the power and conviction of Her words and voice: "She drove back evil hap, She pronounced mighty words of power, She made cunning Her tongue, and Her words failed not. The glorious Isis was perfect in command and in speech."

Whenever someone dares to encroach on your sacred boundaries, invoke the authoritative voice of your inner Lilith and Isis to take a stand for your sovereign rights.

Isis as the Goddess of Womb Wisdom

To support you in honoring the cycles of your path and your own Divine Feminine nature, Isis next blesses you as Yemanya within. Isis too is Goddess of the moon and seas, and embodies the Maiden-Mother-Crone powers of conception, creation, and transformation within your womb.

---

86 George W. MacRae, "The Thunder, Perfect Mind," *Nag Hammadi*, Codex VI, Tractate 2: Protocol of the Fifth Colloquy (1973) The Center for Hermeneutical Studies in Hellenistic and Modern Culture, 1975.

As both Divine Daughter and Mother of the Gods, like Yemanya, Isis is both the innocent receptivity of the Maiden and the creative *shakti* of the Mother.

In "The Thunder, Perfect Mind," Isis describes Herself as being both fertile and barren. Isis is the hopes and dreams that have not yet come to be, or perhaps are not meant to be. She is the countless creations you have already birthed, and the all that is yet to be.

I, myself, have desired to become a mother for quite some time now, and the journey has been one of the greatest initiations of my life. I am both comforted and frustrated by the knowledge that physically my husband and I are very healthy and fertile. And after doing "all the right things" to get pregnant, through deep, painful spiritual work, I have finally come to trust that this has nothing to do with our bodies. I know now that this is a matter of Divine wisdom and timing and not something that we can control or force physically.

Yet I also understand that when we aren't able to manifest what we desire in spite of our best efforts, it is natural for us to feel barren and even betrayed by the Divine in that area of our lives. And I know all too well the profound pain this can bring us. It is why I continue to hold Ereshkigal with such reverence as we have become intimate friends on a journey where the Goddess of grief invites me into Her underworld so often.

But what has helped me continue to feel lush, fertile, and joyful like Inanna, Aphrodite, Yemanya, and Isis is relishing in the gifts and pleasures of my body temple, appreciating how healthy and vibrant I actually am and celebrating all I have and continue to birth. Above all, I have found grace by surrendering to this journey and living as the whole woman and creative, life-giving, flourishing Goddess that I already and truly am.

No matter what part of your life may feel barren, beloved, Isis reminds you that it is okay, natural, and even Divine to have this be. You are a Goddess no matter what has or hasn't come to be for you. You are creative. You are complete. You are Isis.

Like Yemanya, Isis is both the Creatress and the Crone. As Isis proclaims in "The Thunder, Perfect Mind," She is both "the midwife and She who does not bear" and the "solace of (Her) labor pains." Isis is simultaneously the midwife and the mother who strains in Her labor pains. Isis is the Wise Woman who will midwife your dreams into being, providing comfort and healing through the pains of creation. But no matter what you birth or don't, She reminds you to remain content in your own self-containment.

It is worthwhile to note Isis's admission of labor pains, given that the present approach of natural birthing focuses heavily on pain-free and even blissful births, just as much as feminine empowerment messages pose that as women, we can bring forth our dreams solely with ease and joy.

While all women desire a peaceful birthing journey for whatever we are bringing forth, birthing is one of the greatest initiations of our lives. And the initiations that life brings us almost always come with uncertainty, labor, and even pain. The Goddess way is not to fight this, but embrace it. The ease and joy we speak of on the Goddess path does not mean that we won't experience discomfort in our lives. It means that we will accept and ride the waves and surges of our lives, just as we do in labor.

Whether we are birthing a baby or an inspired creation, Isis assures you that laboring is a natural and necessary part of the process. There may be pain and uncertainty. Your patience and faith will be tested. And this is natural. Don't feel like there is something wrong with you or what you are doing. Periods can hurt. Pregnancy can hurt. Labor can hurt. Don't fight the pains, but, like Isis Herself, move through them with surrendered perseverance.

Isis also reminds you that, like Her, you deserve to be supported during any birthing initiation. When Isis gave birth to Horus, She sat alone in the Nile marshes and was agonized by Her labor pains. She squatted down and strained to push Horus out, but to no avail. It wasn't until two Gods came to Her aid and smeared blood (the liquid of life) on Her forehead that She was finally able to birth Horus.

Isis reminds you that even the Goddess of all deities and Divine powers needed support when She struggled to give birth to Her Divine child. So please take the pressure off yourself, beloved. Don't let anyone make you feel like you are less of a woman or Goddess when you, like Isis, are in despair. Instead, allow yourself to be supported like a Queen Goddess, while embracing the natural labor pains of your initiations and creations.

Isis, like Yemanya, is all the cycles of life, death, and renewal that flow through you every moon and during your womanly initiations. She invites you to dance with these sacred rhythms, spiraling through your Maiden-Mother-Crone phases as a whole and empowered Queen.

Isis as the Goddess of Abundance

A Queen is regal and rich, and Isis is here to open you up to receiving your earthly bounty as Pachamama. She is the power within you to manifest material supply through the source of abundance within as She proclaims to Lucius: "I am nature, the parent of things, the Queen of all the elements, the primordial progeny of ages."[87]

---

87 Apuleius, *The Metamorphosis, or The Golden Ass, and Philosophical Works of Apuleius*, trans. Thomas Taylor (London: Sold by R. Triphook and T. Rodd,

She is the primal *shakti* power within you and every woman that can create galaxies. Why ask so little of yourself when you can birth worlds into being, beloved? She is the holy child of the universe that you are. Why settle for so little when you are worthy of all the abundance of heaven and earth?

As Lucius says to Her in his prayer of thanks to Isis: "The hours and seasons return by thy appointment, and the elements reverence thy decree. By thy nod blasts of wind blow, the clouds are nourished, seeds germinate, and blossoms increase."[88]

When you awaken your *shakti* powers, you work with Divine and natural forces to prosper and flourish. When you claim yourself as a Queen, you wear the crown of self-worth, commanding to be respected, supported, and valued in all your majesty.

Isis as the Goddess of Alchemy

Commanding rightful treatment is essential in order for you to own your Wise Woman gifts as you did with Brigid, given the collective traumas that have held us sorceresses back for so long. Alchemy, magic, spiritual knowledge, and healing are some of Isis's most renowned powers, and She will delight in igniting them within you as Brigid has.

Just as we can awaken our latent spiritual gifts on our own healing journeys, Isis transmuted the lead of Her limitations into the gold of magical abilities and spiritual powers, which She used to protect Her son, Herself, and Her people.

It was during Her desperate and grief-filled search for Osiris's corpse that She transformed Herself into a swallow or kite, becoming a Goddess of shape-shifting and transformation.

1822).

88 Ibid.

It was the second time that She recovered all His dismembered parts that She invented embalming, becoming the patron Goddess of death rites and the afterlife.

It was in Her fervent attempt to resurrect Osiris that She grew Her glorious wings, becoming a Goddess of freedom and protection. It was Her ability to revive Osiris through the chanting of spells that made Her the Goddess of *heka* (Kemetic word for magic), *hesi* (sacred chants), ritual, and resurrection.

It was the miraculous conception of Horus during Her tragic, final act of lovemaking with Osiris that turned Her into a Goddess of fertility and one who could change fate.

As a single mother cast out of Her Queendom and living in fear and hiding from Her brother Set, Isis required additional magical power to keep young Horus safe. Her resolve to do so compelled Her to extract the secret name of Her grandfather, the Egyptian sun-God Ra, using the magic and cunning already at Her disposal. In the myth, Isis created a snake whose venom was mixed with Ra's own saliva, making the otherwise invulnerable God susceptible to its poison. She placed the snake on Ra's daily journey. When Ra was stung, Isis watched quietly as all the other Gods failed in Their attempts to relieve Him.

Finally, Isis offered to help, but claimed that She required His real name in order to work Her magic. As the Egyptians believed that one's real name contained one's true power, it was guarded above all treasures. Reluctantly, Ra eventually relinquished His real name, asking that She never reveal it to anyone else (a promise She upheld).

Once She learned His secret name, Isis kept Her word and used Her magic to save Ra. She was then able to use Her amplified powers for Her true aim, and healed Horus of everything from migraines to a deadly scorpion sting as She raised Him on Her own. Along the way, She became revered as the Mistress of charms and enchantments, Lady of incantations, the Great Goddess who heals, Great Sorceress, and Lady of the flame as She used Her gifts to help fellow deities and humans alike.

Her perseverance and dedication ascended Isis to the status of most powerful of the deities in the knowledge of magic and healing.

Isis as your inner Brigid—your inner alchemist, healer, magician, medicine woman, spellcaster, witch, midwife, and Wise Woman—reminds you that through every tragedy and test you face on your path, you will also cultivate greater wisdom, resilience, and power within you that will elevate you to heights you may otherwise never know.

And with each level you rise to, your own spiritual gifts will expand, which you can use to channel miracles for yourself and others. You become, like Isis, the High Priestess who initiates fellow sisters back into their spiritual strength and magical gifts by living from your own.

Isis as the Queen Goddess of All

As the Queen of the celestials, Supreme of all Divinities, Queen of all elements and realms, light of the Goddesses, and Goddess of All, Isis is all of your Divine Feminine powers. She is the luminescent essence of all the Goddesses fused in you.

And Her journey is one of all women. In going through everything, She becomes the Queen of everything. She faces and transcends all initiations, becoming the rightful ruler of all. She reminds you that while neither us women nor the Goddesses themselves are invulnerable to trauma and tragedy, you can transform the greatest pains of your life into your greatest Sacred Feminine gifts.

You can apply them beyond your own life and share them in sacred service and with Divine purpose.

Just as She did with Osiris, when Horus became king of Egypt, Isis continued to lead and serve Her people with grace, wisdom, and love. When Her time came to ascend into the afterlife Herself, She joined Osiris and ruled as Queen alongside him, but in Her own right and with Her own self-directed roles.

As Her powers and worship continued to expand, She became incorporated into new and existing Goddesses all over the world, attaining Her title as Goddess of Ten Thousand (or Infinite/ Endless) Names. What Isis really represents as the omnipresent Goddess, beloved, is your own omnipotent nature as a woman.

When you can own every part of yourself as Divine, you become a powerful leader in the world by way of giving other women permission to claim their sovereignty as well. While you are empowered to become a leader on behalf of any cause you wish, you also don't have to take on any specific worldly role to be a leader. Nor do you need to wait until you feel experienced, credible, or good enough. You lead simply through your own shining example of fully embracing your life lessons and being your true Goddess self.

As you live from your Divine power and inspire fellow women to do the same, you contribute to the resurrection of the Sacred Feminine, the reclamation of the Goddess, and the restoration of sacred sisterhood.

You demonstrate that you don't need any permission outside of yourself to rest in your power to take the lead in your life and to be the all-ruling Queen of your world.

You hold space for us all to shine our light and share our gifts by honoring your own. You inspire us all to rise up as Queens who support and celebrate each other's unique journeys. You become a radiant living vessel for Isis, Goddess of all, to rise again through you and every woman on earth.

It is time now, sister, to wear your crown and take your throne. To sit, like Isis, as the Sovereign Queen in your life and in the world.

Isis on my Mind

Yeye Luisah Teish

Look at Her!
Sitting there on that Throne.
Like She be the Ancient Queen
Like She be the Earth, so green.
Mother with a Thousand Breasts.

Look at Her!
Sitting on that throne.
Like She be the brightest Light.
Like She be the Darkest Night.
The Sparkling Jewel of the Nile.

Look at Her!
Sitting there on that Throne.
Like She be the Everything.
Like She be the outstretched wing.
The Great Beginning and the End.

She looks at me.
Looking at Her Throne.
She says to me "I be we".
She says to me "You be me".
She says "Sit down you're home."

For Isis is the mirror.

Isis at the Parliament of World Religions

Lauren Raine

Ritual organized by Macha Nightmare at the
Parliament of World Religions in Salt Lake City in 2015.

Sovereignty: The Original Sin

Trista Hendren

Every time we put out a new anthology, I learn a lot more about each manifestation of Goddess, and I learn a lot more about myself. We were knee-deep in production of this book during the outbreak of COVID-19. I spent the first month almost entirely at home, sleeping 14 hours a day and not doing much more than the bare necessities. I made up for years of not sleeping and pushing through—as capitalist patriarchy demands of most women.

But I also released a lot that wasn't mine. Like many of us, I had a major shift during the lockdown, which thankfully, was fairly brief in Norway. My husband noted that I seemed happier, lighter. I told him, *I stopped giving all the fucks!!* I quit only posting photos of myself where I was wearing makeup and my hair was done. Joy became the only important factor in whether or not I would share something.

My dreams became increasingly vivid with my deepened slumber. I faced many of my demons and reconnected with my ancestors—and my pain.

For most of my life, Christianity, and then Islam, covered up my deep insecurities of being a 'bad' person. Mary Oliver's words come to me often:

> *"You do not have to be good.*
> *You do not have to walk on your knees*
> *for a hundred miles through the desert, repenting."*[89]

---

89 Oliver, Mary. *Dream Work*. "Wild Geese." Atlantic Monthly Press; 1st edition, 2014.

As a recovering perfectionist, I am not sure I will ever quite feel good enough. Or well-read enough. Or healed enough. It always seems there is more work to do.

Toko-pa Turner wrote that, "Perfectionism is one of the great pillars of patriarchy, used to stem the rise of the wild feminine. It is an impossible standard that, when we strive for it, guarantees our failure because it's ultimately unreachable... The only antidote to perfectionism is to turn away from every whiff of plastic and gloss and follow our grief, pursue our imperfections, and exaggerate our eccentricities until the things we once sought to hide reveal themselves as our majesty."[90]

During the course of putting out every-single-one of my books, there has been a point where I felt like giving up. That point came to me several months ago, when after a particularly grueling week of editing, I decided to host a beloved brother-friend for a feast at our home. At the end of the day, I realized I was in no condition to cook. I was in the midst of a heavy, painful period. My mind was fried, my body tired. I laid on the couch with my husband and said, *I don't feel like doing this.*

But I after weeks of isolation in lockdown, I decided to rally. As usual, I went way over the top. Our table was plentiful and the food was delicious. It was nice to have company again.

The evening started to go downhill toward the end. I had averted a few passive-aggressive comments over the evening, making excuses because I was tired and did not feel like getting into it. And then I was finally done. I was being taunted about my work by someone who claimed to care about me. Instead of calmly dealing with the first jab, which would probably have stopped him in his tracks—I let it mount, losing my sovereignty by exploding in fury.

---

90 Turner, Toko-pa. *Belonging: Remembering Ourselves Home.* Her Own Room Press; 1st edition, 2017.

This is not a new thing for me. I tend to take it and take it until I blow up. Or, that was my old standby. I have gotten better over the years, but this is still my default when I am tired, sick or worn down. Claiming my sovereignty would have entailed canceling the dinner. Or at the very least, not engaging, and ending the evening early.

But I wanted to be a good hostess. I wanted to be the nice 'big sister.' I ended up being anything but either. Perhaps I needed to hear his words to understand who he really was to me—and figure out why I was still participating in this painful dance.

Terry Tempest Williams wrote that, "The moment Eve bit into the apple, her eyes opened and she became free. She exposed the truth of what every woman knows: to find our sovereign voice often requires a betrayal."[91] For me, this first betrayal was to my father—a relationship dynamic that continues to rear its ugly head when I revert to my childhood submissive-good-girl state.

As I chewed on the interaction with my friend during the following weeks, I started to think about times this has happened in the past with various men. I suppose what has been confusing to me is that these are not "bad" men. But they are patriarchal men—behaving as they were socialized.

Under patriarchy, sovereignty is the greatest betrayal—the original sin. If you look up the antonyms for *sovereign,*[92] they include all the things many of us were groomed to be in the church and/or patriarchal family structure:

- dependent
- limited
- restricted

---

91 Williams, Terry Tempest. *When Women Were Birds: Fifty-four Variations on Voice.* Picador; Reprint edition, 2013.

92 Dictionary.com

- minor
- secondary
- subordinate
- unimportant
- inferior
- submissive
- subservient

Patriarchal men (and their institutions) do not recognize the divinity of women. While I have worked through a lot of this already, I have still tried to validate myself through both at times. But these attempts were just picking at the scab of the wound. True healing comes from recognizing our own divinity—not in validation from others.

When you are raised to worship men, this is a difficult lesson to learn.

I grew up with a paternal Grandma who muttered. She was the perfect hostess, always. But in the kitchen with me, preparing the food, or cleaning up, she would complain to herself. (Sometimes about me.) I am not sure if she knew she was audible or not. I never saw her do it around my dad or grandpa—just the other women in the family.

I did not see my Nano come into her Queendom until after my Pappa died. Just before his funeral, she snapped at me. It caught me off guard, because it was so uncharacteristic of her. I held back the tears (and any response) out of respect for her grief. But after that day, I saw my grandma stop taking care of other people. *She* became the one *we* served.

In retrospect, I am grateful for that day, and whatever emerged in her then. While she loved my grandpa—and they had a good relationship for nearly 65 years—she always deferred to him. After he died, she bowed to no one.

I hope I don't wait until I am 90-years-old to claim my Queendom —fully and unapologetically. My Nano was a wonderful woman. But I have to wonder in retrospect how much of herself she sacrificed over the course of her lifetime to be congenial.

As Toni Morrison wrote in *Sula*, "Being good to somebody is just like being mean to somebody. Risky. You don't get nothing for it."[93] That book was life-changing for me, and yet—I don't know how many times it will take for me to fully absorb its message.

As she was dying, Sula asked her life-long, ever-suffering friend Nell, "How do you know who was good. How do you know it was you? I mean maybe it wasn't you. Maybe it was me."[94]

That passage changed my entire perspective on what it meant to be a woman. Like Nell, I spent most of my life trying to be a *good* girl.

Goddess teaches us to connect with ourselves and with our joy. When we are in that flow, we are sovereign—and by default we are *good enough*. We are always enough. We are allowed to be human and to make mistakes. We are encouraged to look at our darkness and shadows to facilitate our healing, and the fullness of our be-ing.

In *Dreams of Isis*, Nomandi Ellis asks: "How can Isis truly be a goddess worthy of honor when she has these dark tendencies?" She answers, "In a way Isis has been recovering from what Clarissa Pinkola Estés calls a 'Nice-nice' complex. She has spent her life being too good, too kind, and turning the other cheek so often that her head begins to spin. She is the kind of woman who will smile during the day, but by night she howls alone in the dark of

93 Morrison, Toni. *Sula*. Knopf, 1976.
94 Morrison, Toni. *Sula*. Knopf, 1976.

the moon. Women who fear the words of power expend a lot of energy biting their tongues."[95]

When I try to be 'good' by doing what I think other people want me to do, everything goes to shit. That's when my sovereignty goes out the window. But I am learning to stay in my own zone, and each year gets a little better.

A few years ago, I would have written off my male friend entirely. After years of abuse from my children's father, I had absolutely zero energy left for any nonsense from anyone. I had to put space between myself and most men in order to heal. But I realized when I ran into him again that he is not the 'jerk' I had been fuming about—he is someone who reverted to his patriarchal upbringing in a heated debate. And I had reverted to mine.

I did not feel angry anymore when I saw his face. I remembered why I cared for him—and told him as much. He had become the annoying little brother I had always wanted in a city where I have no extended family. He came into my life to teach me something about myself—and for me to teach him as well.

I am a work in progress. We all are. The gift of learning how to garden is that you realize that there is no end-point. No matter how stunning your garden is, there is always more to do—even if it is just upkeep. The weeds are eager to pop back up—and there always will be a few here and there that need tending to. But you also learn that just the small act of pulling weeds every day—and planting beautiful and nourishing plants—eventually results in a glorious yard.

---

95 Ellis, Normandi. *Dreams of Isis: A Woman's Spiritual Sojourn*. Quest Books; 1995.

Embracing Goddess Spirituality has healed so much in me—but She requires us to do the work—and keep up with the weeds. Sue Monk Kidd described it perfectly in *The Book of Longings*:

> "Think of it—the life you're living can be torn apart like Osiris's and a new one pieced together. Some part of you might die and a new self will rise up to take its place.
>
> Do not leave it to fate. You must be the one who does the resurrecting. You must be Isis re-creating Osiris."[96]

My life has been torn apart many times—but none so much as when I became a single mother. I miscarried my third child as my marriage to my children's father was unraveling. At the time, it was devastating—and it has taken me years to get over the loss of what I was certain was a sister for my daughter. I planned to name her Grace—I suppose because that was what I had most wanted my entire life. To receive grace—to be *Grace* incarnate.

A third child as a single mother with my particular circumstances would have tanked me. I can see in retrospect, what I most needed was to complete myself—not raise a third child. The grace —and the sovereignty—I have been searching for was always there within myself, waiting to be claimed.

While I have healed things within myself through birthing and raising my children—I am still in the process of birthing myself—and reclaiming the sovereignty I have fought so hard for them to have.

For me, sovereignty is learning to love and accept ourselves fully—to shed the things that are not ours to carry anymore—the destructive patterns we inherited and sometimes reenact. In doing so, we become the Divine Queens we were meant to be.

---

96 Kidd, Sue Monk. *The Book of Longings.* Viking; 2020.

Sovereignty was stolen from women thousands of years ago. It is not an accident that it is so difficult for many of us to reclaim. For some of us, it takes a lifetime to shed the layers and layers of nonsense that were imposed on us by patriarchy.

Carmel Glenane posed a question in her excerpt that has haunted me since I read it. She wrote, "delve into yourself and ask yourself why you don't consider yourself 'first' in everything."[97]

The more I thought about it, the more angry I became at my own indoctrination. I find putting myself first almost impossible. And that is after decades of work. We are deeply socialized since birth not to do such a 'selfish' thing. We are taught to put every other person and thing ahead of our own needs. Our Great Mother Goddess shows us a different path. The stories, rituals and affirmations outlined in this anthology model how to get out of our heads and reconnect with our hearts.

We weren't meant to do any of this alone. Sitting together face-to-face in women's circles has been one of the best things I have ever done for myself. Through the sharing of our stories, we heal. We see ourselves in the mistakes and triumphs of others. We learn and we grow and we learn to love ourselves in all our messiness. We are given a portal back to our Goddess nature.

I hope you have found such a healing in this book, too.

What a joy it has been to share the journey of so many amazing women learning to soar on the wings of Isis. What a gift to all of us that these contributors have been so generous in sharing what helped them heal through connecting to the sovereign divinity of Auset.

---

97 *The Alchemies of Isis Embodiment through The High Priestess* – Carmel Glenane BA Dip Ed ©2015.

A few months ago, my beautiful circle sister Camilla taught me Fia's song, *Shedding Skins*. The chorus states:

> "I am beautiful and fucked up, in the most glorious way
> When standing in my truth, who cares what people say
>
> 'Cause moment we stop running from the demons
> in our heads and instead we choose to love them
>
> When saying yes to life of shadow and light
> oh, our suffering is done and we come alive"[98]

May our suffering be done—and may we all become *truly* alive. May the *Goddess of Ten Thousand Names* restore the throne that is the birthright of each and every woman.

98 Fia, *Made of Stars.* "Shedding Skins." CD Baby, 2016.

Prayer/Invocation[99]

Syma Kharal

Dua Ast! *Beloved Isis, as Goddess of All within me, thank you for empowering me to sit on the throne of my life as its Sovereign Queen. Help me to wear my crown and own my authority with regal grace.*

Help me to embrace the trials of my life with courage and faith, keeping only the lessons and growth they come to offer. Make me resilient like you so that I may always persevere. I open myself to ascending to the highest heights my soul can reach. I offer myself to be of the greatest service on this earth. Make me a vessel for Divine love, healing, magic, and miracles. Let me recall and re-awaken my Divine Feminine spiritual gifts and use them with reverence for the highest good of all.

Let me lead and inspire as you did. Help me trust and honor my path and gifts and share them wisely and lovingly. Let me be supported as you yourself were. Let me know myself as the All-Goddess that you are, that I am.

Let me spread my wings and soar high like you. Let me love and be loved deeply and completely as you. Let me be all that I am and came here to be, one with you as you are with me. Dua Ast. Dua Ast. Dua Ast. *So be it. So it is.*

---

99 This prayer is from Syma Kharal's book, *Goddess Reclaimed: 13 Initiations to Unleash Your Sacred Feminine Power*, which thoroughly discusses 13 Goddesses and culminates with an extensive chapter on Isis. To compliment the flow of this anthology, we broke the chapter into 4 parts.

Bonus Coloring Sheet

Max Dashu

From: *Deasophy: Coloring Book of Goddesses .:. Spirits .:. Ancestors* - Icons from the Suppressed Histories Archives, with drawings and commentary by Max Dashu .Available from www.veleda.net/deasophy.html

What's Next?!

The next anthology in this series are:

Willendorf's Legacy: The Sacred Body – edited by Trista Hendren, Tamara Albanna and Pat Daly.

Warrior Queen: Answering the Call of The Morrigan – edited by Trista Hendren, Jess Johnson and Pat Daly.

In Defiance of Oppression – The Legacy of Boadicea – edited by Trista Hendren, Joey Morris and Pat Daly.

Anthologies and children's books on the Black Madonna, Mary Magdalene, Mother Mary, Aradia, Kali, Boadicea, Brigid, Sophia, Spider Woman, Persephone and Kuan Yin are also in the works.

Details to be announced.

http://thegirlgod.com/publishing.php

List of Contributors

April C. Heaslip, PhD, is a mythologist and educator who earned her doctorate in Mythological Studies with emphasis in Depth Psychology at Pacifica Graduate Institute. She holds a master's in Social Ecology from Goddard College and a bachelor's in Psychology and Women's Studies from West Chester University after studying at the Universidade Federal de Uberlândia, Brazil.

Uniting interconnected levels of inquiry via Women's Studies, Literary + Film Studies, post-Jungian Psychology and sustainability, her work focuses on applied ecofeminist mythology and the curative powers of creativity and synchronicity. Her forthcoming book with University Press of Mississippi, *Regenerating the Feminine: Chronicling the Radical Rise of the Feminine in Psyche, Culture & Nature,* considers the impact of this monumental resurgence as healing agent across individual, collective, and environmental realms.

Arlene Bailey is an Artist and Author, a mystic with a hunger for the deep end of experience and a woman who howls under the juicy and delicious full moon in ancient ritual. Through visionary art and magical weaving of words and ideas, she creates portals for women who are seeking the raw, the authentic, the wild, the sacred.

Drawing on her experience as an Artist, Writer, Ordained Priestess, Teacher of Women's Mysteries, Wise Woman Herbalist and retired Anthropologist, Arlene's offerings invite women to explore deeper mythologies and ways of being. Listening to their ancient memories and soul knowings, she creates invitations for women to listen to the voice of their Soul while stepping into personal sovereignty.

For more information on current classes and projects, visit: www.arlenebaileyart.com

www.facebook.com/sacredwildstudio
www.instagram.com/arlenebaileyartist

Arna Baartz is a painter, writer/poet, martial artist, educator and mother to eight fantastic children. She has been expressing herself creatively for more than 40 years and finds it to be her favourite way of exploring her inner being enough to evolve positively in an externally focused world. Arna's artistic and literary expression is her creative perspective of the stories she observes playing out around her. Claims to fame: Arna has been selected for major art prizes and won a number of awards, published books and (her favourite) was used as a 'paintbrush' at the age of two by well-known Australian artist John Olsen. Arna lives and works from her bush studio in the Northern Rivers, NSW Australia. Her website is www.artofkundalini.com

Bajra (Ann-Lee Waite) entered into her spiritual and transformational journey when she was 55. The near thirty years of meditation prior was an attempt at being comfortable in the uncomfortable world that said her blackness, femaleness, and sexual trauma made her of less value. Meditation was supposed to make all that bearable, and it almost did... Until her second Saturn return.

In her first return, she joined AA, found a meditation sangha, completed college, and had a son. She would later be directed into the wellness industry.

In her second return she learned of her goddess self and she learned how significantly early trauma influences the personality and the collective, and is much of what needs unraveling in a kundalini awakening. As part of her spiritual journey she has dedicated her remaining years as an earth being to serve, specifically in interrupting the cycle of intergenerational trauma.

Carmel Glenane B A Dip Ed. Owner/Director of Atlantis Rising Healing Centre™ and Mystery School, has studied esoteric and psychological disciplines since 1975. The Atlantis Rising Healing Centre™ is one of only 16 Crystal Tones® singing bowl Temples in the world.

A channelled writer, esoteric teacher and sought after visionary healer, Carmel books include: *The Alchemies of Isis Embodiment through The High Priestess, Awaken Your Immortal Intelligent Heart a Blue Print for Living in the Now, Embodying The Divine Masculine of All Truth, through The High Priest, The Miracle of the Mysteries Revealed through The Hearts Secrets.* Her most recent book, *The Final Secret,* forms the core teaching text for The Divine Feminine Philosophy taught through The Atlantis Rising Mystery Ascension Training programme. Crystal Tones® Advanced Alchemy singing bowls are used in all training and tour programmes.

She is known for her transformative tours, sacred ceremonies and powerful vortex gridding around the world in sacred tour destinations such as: Egypt (17 tours), Japan (4 tours) North, Central and South America, Turkey, Greece, Hawaii Islands, Indonesia, India, and Australia.

With over 25 years experience in the self-development industry, Carmel helps people to facilitate their journey to the Intelligent Heart through the energy of 'The Mothers' wisdom.

Carmel's ecstatic energy, charisma, charm, impactful coaching, and deep belief in her mission turn your dreams to reality.

Christine Shahin is the Founder of Goddess Beauty. Known as the "Beautifier", "Mudder" and "Mudder Goddess" by her friends and community, Christine is a Licensed Cosmetologist, Make-Up Artist, Folk Herbalist & Natural Pigment Hair Colorist; she authored the book *Natural Hair Coloring: How to Use Henna and Other Pure Herbal Pigments for Chemical-Free Beauty* based on her extensive experience using herbs to color hair in her cutting edge wellness beauty, salon/spa Faces of Astarte.

Christine had one the first all natural salons in New York State in her home in 1990, Herbal Hair & Skin Care. Christine was catapulted into activism when her rural agricultural community was sited for a regional landfill and incinerator in 1989; she been an environmental, social justice and human rights activist since, her work recognized by the New York State Labor and Environment Network, *Parents* Magazine, *Parenting* Magazine, Herkimer County Legislature, and The Clinton White House; she was an official delegate to the World Summit on Sustainable Development (WSSD) in Johannesburg South Africa in 2002.

deTraci Regula is head of the Temple of Isis, a legally-recognized church and temple based at Isis Oasis Sanctuary in Geyserville, California. She is presiding Priestess with the Temple of Isis and an Archpriestess of the Archpriesthood Union with the Fellowship of Isis. Her passion is visiting ancient Isis temple sites, expanding the aretalogy of known names of Isis, and connecting others with the great and glorious goddess Isis.

International opera singer, speaker, visionary, ancient wisdom expert and best-selling author **Dominique Oyston** is founder of the Goddess Voice Academy, a platform designed to re-introduce the spiritual, energetic, creative and awakening feminine forces of the voice to modern speakers, leaders and conscious entrepreneurs.

Dominique's dynamic 20-year stage career, magical voice, technical brilliance and powerful intuitive channel, plus 30 years study of mythology and healing, make her a unique teacher of how to authentically serve and inspire.

Dominique guides clients to fully embody their goddess nature and gifts and turn their mission into a luminous message that resonates powerfully to create ripples of change.

Dominique lives in Melbourne, Australia with her two boys where she chats to goddesses, writes, teaches and plans her next revolutionary adventure.

Follow Dominique here: www.goddessvoiceacademy.com/blog
FB page: www.facebook.com/goddessvoice

Donna Snyder founded the Tumblewords Project in 1995 and continues to organize its free weekly workshop series and other events in the El Paso borderlands. A version of her poem "in search of the one who is waiting" is included in her collection of poetry published by NeoPoiesis Press, *The Tongue Has Its Secrets*. Her other books include *Poemas ante el Catafalco: Grief and Renewal* (Chimbarazu Press) and *I Am South* (Virgogray Press). Her poetry, fiction, and book reviews appear in such journals and anthologies as *Red Fez, Queen Mob's Teahouse, VEXT Magazine, Mezcla, Setu, Puerto del Sol, Jesus, Muhammad and the Goddess, Inanna's Ascent, Original Resistance*, and *Speak the Language of the Land*. Snyder previously practiced law representing indigenous people, people with disabilities, and immigrant workers.

Duann Kier is a psychic channeler, hypnotist, ordained minister, spiritual teacher and performer of sacred ceremonies. Her most recent book is *Return of the Divine Feminine, Rise of the Divine Masculine: And the Men Who Are Calling for Her Return*. She is a former Christian fundamentalist with a Master of Religious Education degree from New Orleans Baptist Theological Seminary and is also the author of *Fundamen-Talisman: Resurrecting the Fundamentals of Relationship from the Fundamentalism of Religion*. It has been referred to as a handbook for recovering Christian fundamentalists. Duann lives in rural central Mississippi and created the website www.MetaphysicalMississippi.com to help with the great spiritual awakening going on in the state. You can find out more about her and her work at www.DuannKier.com. Her life and work motto is, "lightening up enlightenment!"

Elisabeth Slettnes is a world-renowned artist living in Lilehammer, Norway. She primarily works with oil and acrylic paintings on canvas. You can see more of Elisabeth's paintings at: www.elisabethslettnes.net

Hayley Arrington is a mythologist and poet. She received her MA in women's spirituality from the Institute of Transpersonal Psychology in Palo Alto, CA, where she wrote her thesis on Celtic sun goddesses. She is a devotee of Pelasgian Hera and a priestess in Temple Sophia. Hayley lives with her family in the greater Los Angeles area. For more information, read her Arthurian Witch blog at loathlylady.wordpress.com.

Hazel DaHealer lives surrounded by family in the beautiful state of South Carolina. She has contributed to *Original Resistance: Reclaiming Lilith Reclaiming Ourselves* and *Inanna's Ascent: Reclaiming Female Power.* Her chosen career helps restore order to the chaos life brings for many. Hazel is embracing her inner Isis as she restores her own life to a more Queenly state of being.

Jessica Morell is a woman living in Sonoma County, CA. She spends her days juggling raising her kids, painting an occasional painting and writing poetry between doing the dishes, weeding the garden and tending to her pregnant clients. www.jessicamorell.com

Jhenah Telyndru has always felt called to dance with joy in that liminal space which straddles the realms of history and myth, of individuality and collectivity, of the seen and the unseen. A creative mystic who loves science and values fact, Jhenah embraces the conscious co-creation of the future, while immersing herself in an impassioned study of the past. The path between, she believes, is where the mysteries are revealed and where true magic happens.

Jhenah holds an MA in Celtic Studies from the University of Wales, Trinity St. David, as well as a BA in archaeology. She is the founder of the Sisterhood of Avalon and serves as Academic Dean and lead instructor of the Avalonian Thealogical Seminary. Jhenah teaches four day retreat experiences around North America and the UK, and facilitates pilgrimages to sacred sites in the British Isles and Ireland through Mythic Seeker Tours. She is a frequent presenter and guest speaker at academic conferences, religious symposia, Women's Spirituality gatherings, and Pagan festivals. A priestess in the Avalonian Tradition, Jhenah has been dedicated to the work of the Holy Isle for almost 30 years, and has been active in the Goddess Spirituality movement since 1986.

Jhenah's published works include *Avalon Within: A Sacred Journey of Myth, Mystery, and Inner Wisdom* (Llewellyn, 2010), *The Avalonian Oracle: Spiritual Wisdom from the Holy Isle* (Schiffer, 2016), *Rhiannon: Divine Queen of the Celtic Britons* (Moon Books, 2018), and *The Mythic Moons of Avalon: Lunar and Herbal Wisdom From the Island of Healing* (Llewellyn, 2019). Her forthcoming works include *Pagan Portals: Blodeuwedd* (Moon Books, 2020) and a third book on Avalon coming from Llewellyn in 2021. Her writing has been featured in fiction and non-fiction anthologies; periodicals, including *PanGaia*, *SageWoman*, *The Beltane Papers*, *Circle Magazine*, and *The Tor Stone*; as well as various datebooks and annuals from Llewellyn, Moon Books, and Ninth Wave Press.

In addition to her formal studies, Jhenah has delved into hermetic science, qabalistic philosophy, transpersonal astrology, archetypal tarot, and depth psychology in an ongoing quest to further her understanding of the Universe as it manifests within and without.

Joey Morris is a Celtic Creatrix and UK-based daughter of The Morrigan. She is an author, creatrix CEO of Starry Eyed Supplies, and co-owner of the What the Flux podcast.

"To become a tempered blade of The Morrigan, one must be baptized in blood and fire. These struggles within my lifetime have led me to become a voice for the voiceless, to reach out to the broken, and to poke the shadows in others so that they might begin to heal.

Such a path is dangerous. But so are we. This is the birth of a wild witch who sees with their 'other eyes' and treads the path of edges, sharp and unusual, but filled with adventure, magick of the liminal and the in-between spaces." – Joey Morris

Within the spiritual landscape, her soul mission is to deepen the understanding of our interconnectedness by both honouring the sacred and exploring the masks of the self through channelling relationships to the Divine through written work, poetry, videos, products, and services.

Rev. Dr. Karen Tate, speaker, author, workshop presenter, and social justice activist, is the radio show hostess of the long-running internet podcast, Voices of the Sacred Feminine on Blog Talk Radio. She has been invited to speak at prestigious events such as the Council for the Parliament of World Religions, American Academy of Religion, CIIS, and other colleges and private institutions. She can be seen in the film, *Femme: Women Healing the World*. Karen has authored three books and curated three anthologies, referred to as the "manifesting a new normal trilogy." Tate is a certified Caring Economy Conversation Leader and Power of Partnership Practitioner with Riane Eisler's Center for Partnership Studies. She has a certification from Smith College in the Psychology of Political Activism: Women Changing the World and she's been named one of the Thirteen Most Influential Women in Goddess Spirituality and a Wisdom Keeper of the Goddess Spirituality Movement. She lives high atop a mountain these days with her husband of 36 years, Roy, and their feline daughter, Lilly, named for the Goddess. You can find her at karentate108@yahoo.com, on Facebook or at her website, www.karentate.net

Kat Shaw prides herself on breaking through the stereotypical views of beauty that have been cast upon society by the media, having made her name painting the glorious reality that is a woman's body.

Her nude studies of real women garnered unprecedented popularity within only a few short months, as women were crying out for themselves to be portrayed in art, rather than the airbrushed images of the perfection of the female form that are so rife in today's culture.

After graduating with a fine art degree, Kat achieved a successful full-time teaching career for 14 years, and continues to teach art part-time whilst passionately pursuing her mission of world domination by empowering as many women as possible to reach their fullest potential by embracing their bodies and loving themselves wholeheartedly.

Kat spreads her inspirational magic through her artwork, her Wellbeing business "Fabulously Imperfect", and her dedication to Goddess energy.

Reiki is a huge part of her life, and as a Reiki Master, Kat is committed to sharing Reiki, teaching Usui, Angelic and Karuna Reiki, and channelling Reiki energy through her artwork to uplift and heal.

As a Sister of Avalon, Kat also works directly with her Goddess consciousness, connecting to Goddess and Priestess energy and translating it into Divine Feminine infused paintings to inspire women and spread Goddess love.

Kat is also mum to a gorgeous teenage daughter, a bellydancer and an avid pioneer to improve the lives of rescue animals.

Katherine Skaggs is a visionary artist, intuitive, spiritual teacher, author and painter of souls. Guided to merge her intuitive, spiritual path with her art in the early 90s, Katherine has emerged as an internationally known visionary artist over the years since. Goddesses, Angels, Ascended Masters and many Divine Beings of Light all grace the canvas and heart of Katherine. In addition to these beautiful Light Beings who transmit messages of love and wisdom through their presence, Katherine has painted and channeled guidance for 1000s of soul portraits and spirit guide paintings.

Credits as Artist include:
The Mythical Goddess Tarot, Pocket-full of Goddesses: A Blessing Oracle; plus more than 80 altar cards.

Credits as Artist Author include:
Pocket Blessings Cards; 50 plus altar cards born; soon to come *Masters of Light Wisdom Oracle*.

Credits as Author include:
Artist Shaman Healer Sage.

Lauren Raine, MFA, has been creating visual and performance art about the Great Mother since the early 80's. She studied sacred mask traditions in Bali, and exhibited at Buka Creati Gallery in Ubud, Bali. Her collection of "contemporary Temple masks" devoted to worldwide stories of the sacred feminine, The Masks of the Goddess, traveled throughout the U.S. for over 20 years used by dancers, ritualists and storytellers, and venues included the Chapel of Sacred Mirrors, the International Mask Symposium, the New College of California, and the Parliament of World Religions. In 2007 she received a Fellowship with the Alden Dow Creativity Center at Northwood University and a Puffin Grant for her "Spider Woman" Community Arts Project. In 2009 she was resident artist at the Henry Luce Center for the Arts at Wesley Theological Seminary in Washington, DC. Currently she works in ceramic sculpture and teaches at the Tucson Clay Co-op. www.laurenraine.com www.masksofthegoddess.com

Lydia Ruyle, also known as Ya-Ya, was an 81-year old crone and matriarch who passed away in March 2016. She was an artist and scholar who had been pursuing Goddess research for decades. Her Goddess Banners depict sacred images of the Divine Feminine from the many cultures of the world. Since 1995, the icons have become spirit banners, which flew around the globe weaving the sacred energies of the Divine Feminine. Her research into sacred images of women took her around the globe. She created and exhibited her art, did workshops and led women's journeys throughout the U.S. and internationally. Lydia was the author of two books. *Goddesses of the Americas* was published in 2016 and *Goddess Icons* was published in 2002.

How did Lydia find the Goddess? She called her and she listened. The Goddess asked her to listen, see, touch, learn, laugh, cry and share with art, stories and sacred places of Mother Earth.

Over 30 years ago, she began collecting images of women from art history, which she taught at the University of Northern Colorado in Greeley, Colorado. In 2010, the university created the Lydia Ruyle Room of Women's Art to continue Lydia's mission to teach. In March 1987, an art exhibition at the Loveland Museum and Gallery in Loveland, Colorado called "Better Homes & Goddesses" was the first display of Goddess icons, born for National Women's History Month. In 1993, Lydia invited other women to travel to sacred places with Goddess tours in England, Wales, and Cornwall. Over 300 women joined her to travel in 14 countries.

Lydia made her first Goddess Banners in the series for an exhibition in 1995 at the Celsus Library in Ephesus, Turkey where they flew and spread their energies throughout the month of July. The banner collection grew from 18 to over 300. She used them to empower, teach, and share their stories at sacred sites in 38 countries.

Lindsay goes by the Nom de Plume '**M^h**'; mind 'to the power of' the heart. M^h is a Creative Writer who often refers to herself as a truth-seeking, soul-searching storyteller. She believes in the power of words to perceive, create, and destroy all forms of life. Ultimately she is concerned with the human condition and this is evident in all its forms in her work. Her work that allows her to somehow feel a thing or two, deeply, without judgment. To speak when no one else will.

She has recently debuted her Poetry Chapbook of this nature, titled, simply – *Human Nature* followed up by another provocative collection; *Of Lilith and Delilah*.

Luisah Teish is a storyteller-writer, an artist-activist and spiritual guidance counselor. She is an initiated elder (Iyanifa) in the Ifa/Orisha tradition of the West African Diaspora.

She is the author of *Jambalaya: The Natural Woman's Book of Personal Charms and Practical Rituals*, and she co-authored *On Holy Ground: Commitment and Devotion to Sacred Land* with Kahuna Leilani Birely. Her most recent work is *Spirit Revealing, Color Healing*, a book of Zen Doodles.

She has contributed to 35 anthologies, notably *Spiritual Guidance Across Religions: A Sourcebook for Spiritual Directors and Other Professionals Providing Counsel...* by Rev. John R. Mabry Ph.D., Dan Mendelsohn Aviv Ph.D., Mans Broo Ph.D. and Rev. Cathleen Cox MAT MDiv (Apr 1, 2014) And magazines such as *Ms., Essence,SageWoman*, and the *Yoga Journal.*

She has articles and artwork in Coreopsis: Journal of Myth and Theater, and the Cascadia Subduction Zone Journal of Speculative fiction.

Her performance credits include:
Concert for All Beings, Marin Civic Center (2014); Resonant Streams: An Ancient Call. St. John the Divine Cathedral, New York (2011); The Praises for the World Concert, directed by Jennifer Berezan, Edge of Wonder Music. (2005) She has performed in Europe, Venezuela, New Zealand and the United States.

She teaches online courses, provides editorial assistance, facilitates conferences and weekend workshops, and performs in theaters worldwide.
https://www.yeyeluisahteish.com/
https://ileorunmilaoshun.com/

Max Dashu is a land-walker and history sibyl who uses images to teach women's global history and heritages. Her legendary slideshows bring to light women of power who have been hidden from view, from ancient icons to female leaders, culture-makers, rebels, and medicine women. In 1970 Dashu founded the Suppressed Histories Archives to research women in the global cultural record. From her collection of over 30,000 images, Dashu has created and presented hundreds of slideshows at universities, women's centers, bookstores, conferences, festivals, libraries, prisons, museums, and schools. She has presented at international conferences in Italy, Switzerland, Britain, Australia, Germany, Mexico, Bulgaria, Guatemala, and the US. She also teaches via webcasts, online courses, audio podcasts, her blog Veleda, and via daily Suppressed Histories posts on Facebook. Some of her videos are now available as stream on demand via the Suppressed Histories Portal on Teachable.

Max is the author of *Witches and Pagans: Women in European Folk Religion*, the first volume to be published from her sourcebook Secret History of the Witches. Her most recent publication is the Deasophy Coloring Book. The next is *Pythias, Melissae and Pharmakides: Women in Hellenic culture*, on women's ceremonial culture as well as the roots of rape culture and colonial domination. Max has produced two dvds: *Woman Shaman: the Ancients* (2013) and *Women's Power in Global Perspective* (2008). She is also an artist whose paintings are well known in the women's spirituality community.

Website: https://www.suppressedhistories.net/
Facebook: https://www.facebook.com/Suppressed-Histories-Archives-333661528320/

YouTube: https://www.youtube.com/user/maxdashu/
New Stream-on-Demand Videos: https://suppressed-histories.teachable.com/

Monica Rodgers is an un-fatiguable advocate for the full actualization of Women. She is a champion for advancing consciousness and personal accountability through co-active coaching and women's circles, retreats, and online courses. She is dedicated to helping women live a life of radical self-approval and personal truth, while holding a vision for what is possible when we each do our inner work to fully integrate both our human aspects and our divine.

As a leadership coach, Monica empowers women to awaken from the trance of unworthiness. Her clients become free to guide their businesses and lives with intention, inner strength, flow and ease. Bringing an infectious warmth and playful levity wherever she goes, Monica gives women permission to get messy as they explore their gritty, emotional, intuitive and unknown parts within. Understanding this as their natural habitat, her clients can take action towards realizing their dreams and desires.

With over 25 years of experience in healing modalities, leadership and Co-Active Coaching, she also has a wealth of experience as a writer, blogger, entrepreneur, and business consultant.

Monica is also the founder of Little Bits by Monica Rodgers, and *The Earth Savers Gang* Story Book Series, Revelation Media, and has been featured in: *In Style Magazine, The Today Show*, and *The New York Times.*

Nuit Moore is a witch and priestess whose work and temple serve the Goddess and Her return to the collective consciousness, focusing especially on the empowerment of women, the return of the Goddess temple, and the potent medicine of her path and teachings. Although she comes from mystic traditions from both sides of her bloodline, she began her personal path as priestess in the Dianic and Wise Woman traditions, and is also an ordained priestess with the Fellowship of Isis. Nuit has offered classes and ceremony on female wicce, women's rites/rights, the harvest mysteries, trance arts, wise woman ways, serpent/shakti power, ceremonial movement and sound, liminal magick and ritual theater, etc., for over 25 years, and travels frequently bringing temple and ceremony to festivals and communities. She has been a visionary/channel of the menstrual mysteries and eco-menstruation movement since 1991, and is a long standing weaver of the web of women's blood mysteries. Much of her work as an eco-feminist activist is in connection with her teachings on eco-menstruation. Nuit is also a performance artist/sacred dancer, ceremonial visual artist, and founder of the Ishtar Noir Ritual Theater collective – and is the creatrix of Shakti Goddess Arts (www.shaktistudios.etsy.com) which carries her altar art and ceremonial offerings, wise women herbals, crystals, and her writings. Her website can be found at www.scarletshakti.com and she is also on Facebook at: Nuit Moore, The Scarlet Shakti and on Instagram @thescarletshakti

Olivia Church possesses BA and MA degrees in Egyptology and is working toward a PhD in Historical Studies researching contemporary Goddess Spirituality. As well as a scholar, Olivia is a Pagan witch and Fellowship of Isis Priestess. She is primarily dedicated to the Goddess Aphrodite, as well as several other ancient Mediterranean Goddesses. Olivia has explored the mythology and worship of Aset in her publication for the Pagan Portals series, *Isis: Great of Magic, She of 10,000 Names*.

Pat Daly (editor) is a mother of three daughters and proud grandma. A published author / writer on career and job search issues, Pat lives in Portland, Oregon.

Sharon Putnam is a geologist and web designer who is continually learning new things. Having been raised as a Unitarian Universalist, she was encouraged to explore many spiritual belief systems. Sharon enjoys rock collecting, reading, having fun with friends, spending time at the beach and in the woods, and cooking. Sharon currently resides in Massachusetts and her web site is http://www.DesignBy79.us

Sharon Smith is a writer, ghost writer, editor, and proofreader with a passion for helping women reconnect with their Authentic Selves and Voices. She loves & honors the Great Mother in all Her many forms, and has a deep connection to Nature. She identifies as a Green Witch and follows an eclectic spiritual path that is a blending of Native American and Celtic Teachings, both in her ancestral line.

Sudie Rakusin is a visual artist, sculptor, author, illustrator and publisher. Born and raised in Washington, DC, she currently resides in Hillsborough, NC. Sudie received her BFA in painting from Boston University and her MFA in Painting from the University of Arizona. Being an animal activist and feminist, her artwork flows from what moves her and from where she finds beauty: women, animals, the earth, color, pattern and light. Sudie's art represents the deep connection she feels with these elements. Through her artwork she creates the world as she would like it to be, where harmony exists between animal and human, and where nature thrives. Her work includes pen and ink, papier-mâché sculptures, vessels, abstracts in cold wax and oil, and 3-dimensional oil paintings. Her paintings test the boundaries of what a "painting" is. These works are created on a free form canvas and involve papier-mâché sculpture, beadwork, and mixed media. Her website is www.sudierakusin.com info@sudierakusin.com

Susan Morgaine is a Priestess, Reiki and Crystal Healer, Witch, Writer, and Teacher. She is entering her 22nd year teaching Kundalini Yoga and Meditation, being a Certified instructor through the Kundalini Research Institute.

She is a Certified Women's Empowerment Coach/Facilitator through Imagine A Woman International, founded by Patricia Lynn Reilly. She has long been involved in Goddess Spirituality and Feminism, teaching classes and workshops, including Priestessing local Red Tents.

She is a monthly columnist with PaganPages.org. Her writings can be found in The Girl God anthologies, *Whatever Works: Feminists of Faith Speak* and *Jesus, Mohammad and the Goddess*, as well as Mago Publications *She Rises, Volume 2*, and *Celebrating Seasons of the Goddess*. She is the author of *My Name is Isis, the Egyptian Goddess,* part of the My Name is series of children's books by Girl God Books. She has also been published in *Jareeda* and *SageWoman* magazines.

Susan is an Apprentice Traditional Herbalist, studying for her full Certification and brews her own herbal medicines and body products.

She is a member of the Sisterhood of Avalon. Her website can be found at MysticalShores.com

Syma Kharal is an international Sacred Feminine coach, healer, speaker, retreat leader and #1 Amazon bestselling author of the books *Goddess Reclaimed* and *Manifest Soulmate Love*. She holds an honors degree with distinction in psychology and a certificate in counseling from the University of Toronto, and is a certified Reiki Master, Yoga and Meditation teacher, Spirit Guide and Akashic Records coach. She is dedicated to empowering soulful women heal their deepest wounds, manifest their boldest dreams and flourish in every way.

Syma immersed herself in the healing arts at the age of 14 to overcome the deeply damaging effects of extensive abuse and trauma. In addition to healing herself, her intensive spiritual work led her to co-create a life she never dreamt possible: leaving a toxic corporate career to follow her calling, manifesting and marrying her soulmate, transforming women's lives through her heart's work, and traveling the world with her beloved husband.

She loves nothing more than supporting fellow sisters to do the same—to transcend disempowering patterns, reclaim their full feminine power, and step fully into the Goddesses they truly are.

Visit Syma at: www.FlourishingGoddess.com
Connect with her on:
Facebook: www.facebook.com/FlourishingGoddess
Instagram: www.instagram.com/FlourishingGoddess
YouTube: www.youtube.com/FlourishingGoddessTV

Talia Segal is best known for writing fantasy fiction, and has a fashion blog with international readership (wildroma.wordpress.com). Her poem "The Underworld" was published in the feminist anthology *Inanna's Ascent*, edited by Trista Hendren, Tamara Albanna, and Pat Daly. Talia played roller derby under the name Riot Gere, and now writes graphic novels, reads tarot cards, designs knitting patterns, and obeys the directives of her cat. Her writing can be found for free at Patreon.com/taliasegal.

Tara Reynolds is an artist, tarot reader and spiritual advisor who lives with her two feline familiars in Orlando, FL. You can find more of her work at theawakenedoracle.com

Tracy Andryc is an artist, Veriditas Certified Labyrinth Facilitator, Certified Birth Doula, Reiki Master, Ordained Minister, and the owner and founder of One Path Labyrinth Ventures (www.onepathlabyrinth.org). For over two decades, she has facilitated workshops/rituals and sold her art at venues throughout New England and New York.

Trista Hendren is the Creatrix of Girl God Books. She lives in Bergen, Norway with her family. You can learn more about her projects at www.thegirlgod.com

Tyreesha Garrett is Afro-Indigenous from Cheyenne and Arapaho Tribes, Oklahoma. She is a mother in the Pacific Northwest. Becoming a Mother opened a part of her to reflect and look deeper into her Cultural Identity & Spirituality. Through Self-taught education she came to a Greater Awareness of the impact settler colonialism (Through Terrorist Acts) & the settler colonial system she grew up in. She has sought out to Decolonize her & her children's way of being as to Reclaim their Cultural Identity of being Indigenous as their Culture is their Medicine.

Trista's Acknowledgments

I would like to acknowledge my co-editors. My mother, **Pat Daly,** has edited each and every one of my books. There would be no Girl God Books without her enormous contributions. I was thrilled to also work with one of my dear sister-friends, **Susan Morgaine,** on this project as well—who inspired my interest in Isis/Auset.

I want to give special thanks to several of our contributors. To **Olivia Church** for helping me research and re-work the introduction. Also to **Sharon Smith** for letting me bounce ideas off her—and for her valuable insights. And, to **Arlene Bailey** for her extensive help and emotional support.

I also want to acknowledge the significant contributions of **Tyreesha Garrett**, who opened my eyes to the importance of the naming of our beautiful Goddess.

Tremendous gratitude to **Elisabeth Slettnes** for being a part of this project from the beginning and allowing us to feature her gorgeous full-sized mirrored painting as the cover art.

Many thanks to **Jhenah Telyndru** for taking time out of her busy schedule to write the beautiful Foreword to this anthology.

Enormous appreciation to my husband **Anders Løberg**, who designed the cover, prepared the document for printing and helped with website updates. Your love, support and many contributions made this book possible.

My mom and I would also like to acknowledge her wonderful partner, **Rick Weiss,** for being an all-around awesome guy—and helping us with the page numbers.

Lastly, I would like to thank my dear-sister **Tamara Albanna** for her daily support, love and inspiration. And, to acknowledge **Alyscia**

Cunningham for always being right there to cheer me on in the spirit of true sisterhood.

Thank you to all our readers and Girl God supporters over the years. We love and appreciate you!

Susan's Acknowledgments

I would like to acknowledge the Goddess and her Sisters in the Sisterhood of Avalon.

If you enjoyed this book, please consider writing a brief review on Amazon and/or Goodreads.

Printed in Great Britain
by Amazon